SHUNGITE

SHUNGITE
Expect Miracles

Purifying humanity to reconnect to its divinity with quantum, rule breaking C60 Fullerenes.

An Artist's journey joining the dots between mysterious Shungite, science, geometry and art with keys to our hidden ability to create a miraculous future.

AUTHOR AND ARTIST C SPRAY
EDITED BY SUSIE SYKES

Shungite: Expect Miracles © Copyright 2024 Cassie l Limb

All rights reserved. No part of this publication may be reproduced, distributed or transmitted in any form or by any means, including photocopying, recording, or other electronic or mechanical methods, without the prior written permission of the publisher, except in the case of brief quotations embodied in critical reviews and certain other non-commercial uses permitted by copyright law.

Although the author and publisher have made every effort to ensure that the information in this book was correct when going to press; the author and publisher do not assume and hereby disclaim any liability to any party for any loss, damage, or disruption caused by errors or omissions, whether such errors or omissions result from negligence, accident, or any other cause.

Adherence to all applicable laws and regulations, including international, federal, state and local governing professional licensing, business practices, advertising, and all other aspects of doing business in the UK, US, Canada or any other jurisdiction is the sole responsibility of the reader and consumer.

Neither the author nor the publisher assumes any responsibility or liability whatsoever on behalf of the consumer or reader of this material. Any perceived slight of any individual or organisation is purely unintentional.

The resources in this book are provided for informational purposes only and should not be used to replace the specialised training and professional judgement of a health care or mental health care professional.

Neither the author nor the publisher can be held responsible for the use of the information provided within this book. Please always consult a trained professional before making any decision regarding treatment of yourself or others.

The statements herein are not intended to diagnose, treat, cure or prevent disease. The information provided is for enjoyment and educational purposes only and is not meant to substitute for the advice provided by your doctor or other health care professional.

There are many references in this book to external sources, some with a URL link. At the time of writing, all links were valid. However, this is the internet, and things can and do change frequently. Therefore, if you find a broken link, just search for the source document by name.

For more information, email oraphimcassie@gmail.com
ISBN: 979-8-89316-184-7 - paperback
ISBN: 979-8-89316-185-4 - ebook
ISBN: 979-8-89316-939-3 - audiobook
Inprint name: selfpublishing.com

Dear *YOU*, as you are the reason this book has been written.
(With muttering utterances from Rich Spray)

*"There are only two ways to live your life.
One is as though nothing is a miracle.
The other is as though everything is a miracle."
Albert Einstein.
"Expect Miracles"* with Shungite

Miracle

A **miracle** is an event that is still inexplicable by natural or scientific laws (of which there are many and may you experience them often)

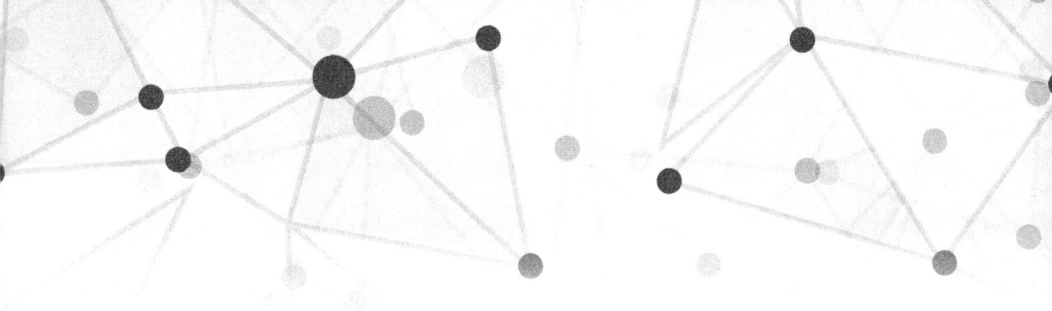

ABOUT THE ARTISTS

Shungite inspired artists are Cassie and Rich and their work can be found at: www.oraphimshungite.com and www.oraphimstudios.com

Why has Shungite remained such a mystery for so long? In this book the magical inner workings of it's remarkable Nobel Prize winning fullerene C60 molecules are opened up for you to connect with on a whole new quantum level of understanding. With the coincidence of a prophesied extra-terrestrial blue glowing explosion linked to the revealing of centuries of control of the entire populace of Earth, Shungite exploded into all our lives.

Our existence is saturated with poisons which Shungite provides the powerful free radical balancing as well as potentially being the key to the unlocking of our innate abilities beyond our wildest dreams. Hailed the total detoxification solution of the century, Shungite purifies, reprogrammes and transforms lives from Electromagnetic smog to radioactive water. You are the key to initiating the global shift in consciousness that Shungite has come to activate in each and every one of us. As Shungite purifies the water we drink we become purified and connected to the Divinity of our humanity, what links us all is Pure Water and there's no stopping the wave of mass awakening now.

CONTENTS

About the Artists vii
Introduction. xi

SECTION 1: Simply Shungite and Energy Systems

1 An Oraphim Exploration of Elite and Black Plain Shungite 3
2 Harmonising Harmful Frequencies 17
3 The Positive Side of Electromagnetic Fields. 27
4 The Significance of 'Waves' 37
5 Fullerenes Past, Present and Future 45
6 Shungite Powder and Purifying Stones for Everyday Health . . .57
7 The Art of Dowsing: Shungite Effects the Energy Body 65
8 Superior Silver Activated Shungite. 71
9 Breaking the Laws of Physics: The Modern Mystery 79

SECTION 2: The Wonder Filled World of Water and Shungite Purification

1 Simply - What is Water? 89
2 Imitating Nature: Water Purification and Distillation 109
3 Radioactive Toxic Water Clean Up 117
4 Capturing the Quantum - Shungite Surprises 121
5 Homoeopathy and Quantum States of Healing. 125
6 Quantum Remineralisation and Bio-Balancing 133

7 Minerals On The Mind; How Does Shungite Do It?........139
8 Your Body the Vehicle for Your Soul 151
9 Shungite Body Care: A Magical Partnership 157
10 Shungite Eye Masks and Their Benefits.................167

SECTION 3: Shungite Transforming Tyrannical Times

1 The Battle for Your Attention, Time, Hearts and Minds 171
2 Survival of the Soul and the Shungite Detox...............179
3 The Blue Star Kachina: A World Changing Event..........185
4 The Hidden Histories 191
5 Have We Been Denied The Knowledge? 199
6 The Rise of Shungite in the Age of the Industrial Revolution .203
7 Soul Development - Shungite the Personal Old
World Rule Breaker 211
8 Oraphim Orgone Developments........................219
9 New Platonic and Pyramid Power......................225
10 Silver Activated Magnetic Shungite Transformations.......231
11 Transitioning Times to Greatness......................237
12 The Limitless Potential - A Glimpse into the Future 243
13 Story Time - Science Finally Catches up with Folklore 247
14 Extra Special Shungite Transformations.................253

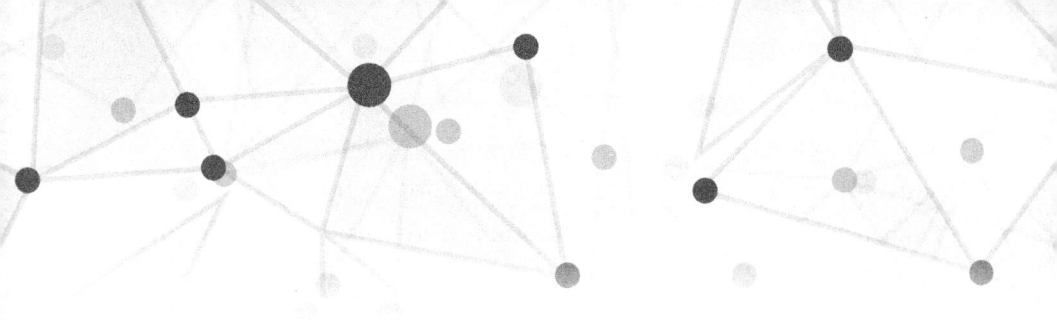

INTRODUCTION

This book is a comprehensive guide that covers many practical ways of using Shungite to enhance your experiences here on our shared planet, with down to earth- fully comprehensible explanations of scientific insights including the latest in quantum physics, really don't worry you will glow with new inner knowledge the way Cassie has broken it down for you; Shungite information can be contradictory but you will learn why, along with how it breaks all the rules to be able to assist you in a myriad of vastly different ways. With this book you will be up to date with the latest facts, findings and deeper mysteries that surround this miraculous stone.

Shungite surprises and delights wherever it is found with life enhancing and even saving effects, from easy detoxification methods desperately needed in our current technologically saturated and poisoned times, our need to detoxify on many levels is paramount and with the potent biofield enhancements it can instantly provide you with, you're able to become the best you can be, ready for the new transformational planetary frequency upgrade that is due around tea time!

You will be guided through your ability to experience 'quantum shifts' in consciousness that must happen for each of us to release us from negative emotional programming ready for the transition into being 'quantum' observational light beings, and this is far easier with the vital help of Shungite; it's simply the one stone for our times that can be used to achieve *bliss and balance*, allowing you to become the best and calm version of yourself amidst the madness of tyrannical megalomaniacs who think they run the system with our consent.

Your journey through these pages is also about revealing who you really are in this current age of chaos and distraction, this journey will lead you to an alchemical and metaphysical transformation that you've been secretly planning and preparing for all this time. Learning how to activate the shifting states through quantum questioning, this journey will give you many opportunities to radiate your desires and wishes from a healed heart state and watch as you magically and magnetically manifest into your life- your true heart's desires for those you love.

Shungite is the key to unlocking miracles, starting with you, so we will begin on the day it began in Sheffield for Cassie where her heart poured out in search for answers to sadly a common problem plaguing modern life: Cancer; is there a cure being kept from us?

Diseases including cancers are a lucrative business and the odds of survival into old age with a disease free passing into the afterlife could well be actively engineered. Cassie had a life changing experience which opened her eyes to the truth about how medical and pharmaceutical companies profit from patients' misfortunes, with the fact that *all* promotion of natural healing protocols are actually illegal, this being a major blocking factor to finding natural alternative options and many who dare to inform the public have even been prosecuted or worse. Cassie, an artist commissioned to deliver public engagement multimedia projects with Sheffield University academics witnessed a medical professional turning away from the son of a former patient's miraculous recovery testimonial and Cassie became determined to learn more. Why did they walk away? Why were they not intrigued and excited to learn what had cured their patient? Could Cassie use her creative skills to help others? Could they be combined and used in a healing way she wished?

That night she asked - *"Dear God, please use me to help others, please guide me to find real solutions, and make my creative skills be used fully to heal and help others."*

As she delved deeper into cancer research Cassie discovered that unconventional and more natural methods of cancer treatment were often discredited and even blocked by the mainstream medical and education system, and that funding for research institutes could be jeopardised by actually finding or knowing of a cure, let alone it being unlawful to actually advertise anything natural as being able to cure cancer.

Cassie had contributed creatively and led the coordination of projects collaborating with many academics and artists, one such commission entitled GTAC (Gaming Technology Against Cancer) where together they were producing interactive sculptures and activities including educational animations and a ground-breaking computer game which was simulating all the elements of Myeloma a 'fatale' bone cancer, with their work being instrumental in the success of raising public awareness of the stages of Myeloma bone cancer treatment and it's harmful side effects.

In this book you'll be introduced to a multitude of scientists and academics that prove the impossible and bring Cassie's wishes to many lives; where academia stops - the creators began producing real life Shungite solutions. You'll also meet many individuals who have benefited from that single prayer and learn how to utilise Shungite as a powerful prophylactic and bioenergy enhancer, dis-ease balancer. Cassie discovered that this miraculous stone will not only help you but also those around you rapidly and without any negative side effects either.

This miracle-making mineraloid called 'Shungite' is now causing a stir in the scientific and medical communities and is the game changer that cannot be stopped in more ways than one. It's important to see how so many harmful poisons have made there way into our lives and how this has all come to pass, with the key factors of exploring the modern control mechanisms of medical, religious and governmental tyranny, you will be shown in an empowering way that you can fully engage in the rewriting of our Earth's survival and humanities development going forward.

Due to Cassie and Rich having worked with the Nobel prize winning element known as the Fullerene Carbon 'C60' for many years they were in a unique situation to fully comprehend Shungite's mission and understand the relevant research they bring to you today with the latest discoveries in science through the quantum reactions of a rare Russian rule breaking carbon.

That fateful evening when Cassie prayed for help she had been heard. She was so full of emotion that night, she remembers how she had been shocked by experiencing the medical establishments' failure to want to know the answers that they claimed they were striving for, which in turn could provide necessary assistance to those in need reaching far into the future; but there is one other important issue too, her concern that the Hippocratic oath to 'Do No Harm' may not be being upheld, in a very major way.

When will this cycle be broken? - She thought with a questioning hope in her heart.

We must examine fundamental questions such as: why are people getting sicker generation after generation? And what can each one of us do about it in reality?

The little known 'Cancer Act' of 1939 outlaws advertising natural treatment options which protects the pharmaceutical industry and mainstream educational institutes incomes, leaving inexpensive natural remedies underutilised and the promotion of them actually illegal.

Whilst this may answer the question as to why we don't have much knowledge of effective natural medicines, what can each of us do to reverse it and make sick people thrive again?

With recent legislation given Royal Assent in 2023 the UK's 'On-Line Safety Bill' is directly impacting the publishing of truth and facts, you used to have every right to educate yourself to a new level of understanding on any given topic, sadly it has now become unlawful to share the whole breadth of research with you today, as in many aspects of coving this topic with evidence based information the 'reader' may be 'up-set' and this is now classified as 'mal-information' and now deemed punishable; what was publish before as evidence based research with facts is disallowed today and this is pure censorship where 'Truth' is the first victim of war.

Cassie had built up a pronominal catalogue of work regarding her public engagement projects which combined art with cutting edge scientific and academic research to educate and engage with the public, inspiring interaction and knowledge growth. She was collaborating with highly regarded academics including Professor's

Kate Phal, Jane Hodson and Fiona Boissonade, as well as Dr's Andy Chantry, Laura Ferraiuolo, and Caroline Evans.

Unconventional approaches in research, project delivery and public engagement is Cassie's specialism and with her unorthodox journey it is a testament to the power of her creativity and off the wall approaches to many situations in the face of adversity that sets her apart and this is both her talent and her strength in achieving and delivering inspiring installations that captured the imaginations of thousands of visitors.

Cassie's long-standing involvement in Sheffield's vibrant creative arts scene saw her collaborate with other skilled and talented artists at The Garden Rooms, International Arts and Science festivals and Kiac Studios as well as receiving awards from many commissioners, funders including the Arts Council (England). Her passionate pursuit covering creative research into brand new platonic solid discoveries, Metaphysics, Meta Language, Law and Inalienable Rights culminated in her Solo exhibition in 2013, yet there seemed to be something completely new and different calling her away from all this.

The potent catalyst for this new creative journey was her discovery of Shungite, which required Cassie and Rich to have made the vacuum in their existing careers and lifestyles for, thus opening a whole new chapter in their lives, bravely they did just that (they both had a deep trust in something unseen) and they became filled with awe and wonder at what they found, the galaxy's fundamental building block and Nobel Prize winning element - the mighty but tiny full of potential - fullerenes, these are found in Shungite and they had a much bigger role to play than they could have ever imagined.

Whilst listening to Nancy L Hopkins on an obscure internet radio station (Wolf Spirit Radio) Cassie learned about a rare stone from

Karelia, Russia. In 2015, with not much other information available on the internet at the time, she kept tuning into Nancy's radio shows and, as the weeks went by both she and Rich felt the urge to develop something unique, something that could be both helpful and also beautiful, which was not available anywhere, a new future was being birthed through a curious carbon that needed bringing to the UK and beyond.

Both Cassie and Rich's wishes had been answered when they discovered that they could use their creativity to help people heal and provide preventative solutions that were affordable utilising this newly found stone: Shungite.

With a small budget from selling their mobile home, they sourced a direct supplier in Karelia, Russia. Lack of e-commerce experience did not stop them from learning the ropes of on-line selling and they applied to some Mind, Body and Spirit events to attend; they were welcomed with open arms and this started something wonderful.

Nancy L Hopkins, who had been a Wi-Fi warfare officer in the US Military had shared how to optimise Shungite with silver so that its ability to be much more effective against harmful 'smart' mobile phone frequencies than regular Shungite stones was achievable; these and other modern air and water borne toxins are causing damage to our nervous systems and bodies, along with being cited as causing cancers and brain tumours, there was no time to waste as they were free to be creative.

Hopkins had discovered by observing Shungites' interactions with silver that a brand new element in combating Wi-Fi warfare and its damaging effects on the body was possible to a new level of protection and it was better than Shungite working alone; this led Nancy and Walt Silva to develop this into a way to enhance Shungite abilities with powerful silver, making a brand new compound these are classified as 'meta-materials and are capable of providing multi band frequency solution's with quantum 'intelligent' adaptive capacities.

Fortunately Rich and Cassie were already familiar with Shungite's secret to success, as it was discovered to contain the 'fullerene' molecule a few years after it was awarded the Nobel Prize in 1996. Fullerenes and Shungite are now featured in increasingly growing numbers of scientific and medical publications. In the early 2000's Cassie had been inspired to design and build large outdoor structures called 'geo-domes' based on the work of Richard Buckminsterfuller's geometry, and Rich had all the technical skills needed to reproduce what they were learning Shungite could be - the best available electromagnetic field (EMF) solution of our times.

Together Cassie and Rich established 'Oraphim' (Oraphimshungite.com) and began producing a variety of uniquely beautiful Shungite based products and services. Their range developed from simple yet effective phone radiation harmonising stickers for reducing techs harmful effects to unique, beautiful and beneficial wellbeing aids, artworks, ornaments, pyramids, cloud-busters, jewellery and more. They partnered with Susie Ashworth to develop a truly natural, organic, vegan body care range with benefits beyond everyone's expectations; all featuring the magical ingredient which is silver activated Shungite.

Working with this new compound they had little idea of just how revolutionary what they were embarking on was; like many they wished to be free of tyranny and government overreach in our 'civilised' society, they fully understand the principles of a growth economy, that being a successful business is to create a cycle of need, and that perpetual growth is key, with the need to be buying and constantly replacing 'stuff' in our lives, yet Shungite is very different, Shungite in its uniqueness actually breaks this consumerist loop, because it is something extraordinary and exotic, they were led to discover something that is simple and works endlessly into eternity with it's infinite energy, you just don't need to keep replacing it!

Its interactions with you are unique just as you are unique and this 'quantum adaptability' is tailored personally in a unique way to every user it interacts with, once you have a little piece of it, it will work with you forever, but just how is this even possible and why do some sellers disregard this vital unique quality? This and so much more you will comprehend in a very real way, very soon.

Full colour resources are available for free download to accompany the book at www.shungiteexpectmiracles.me

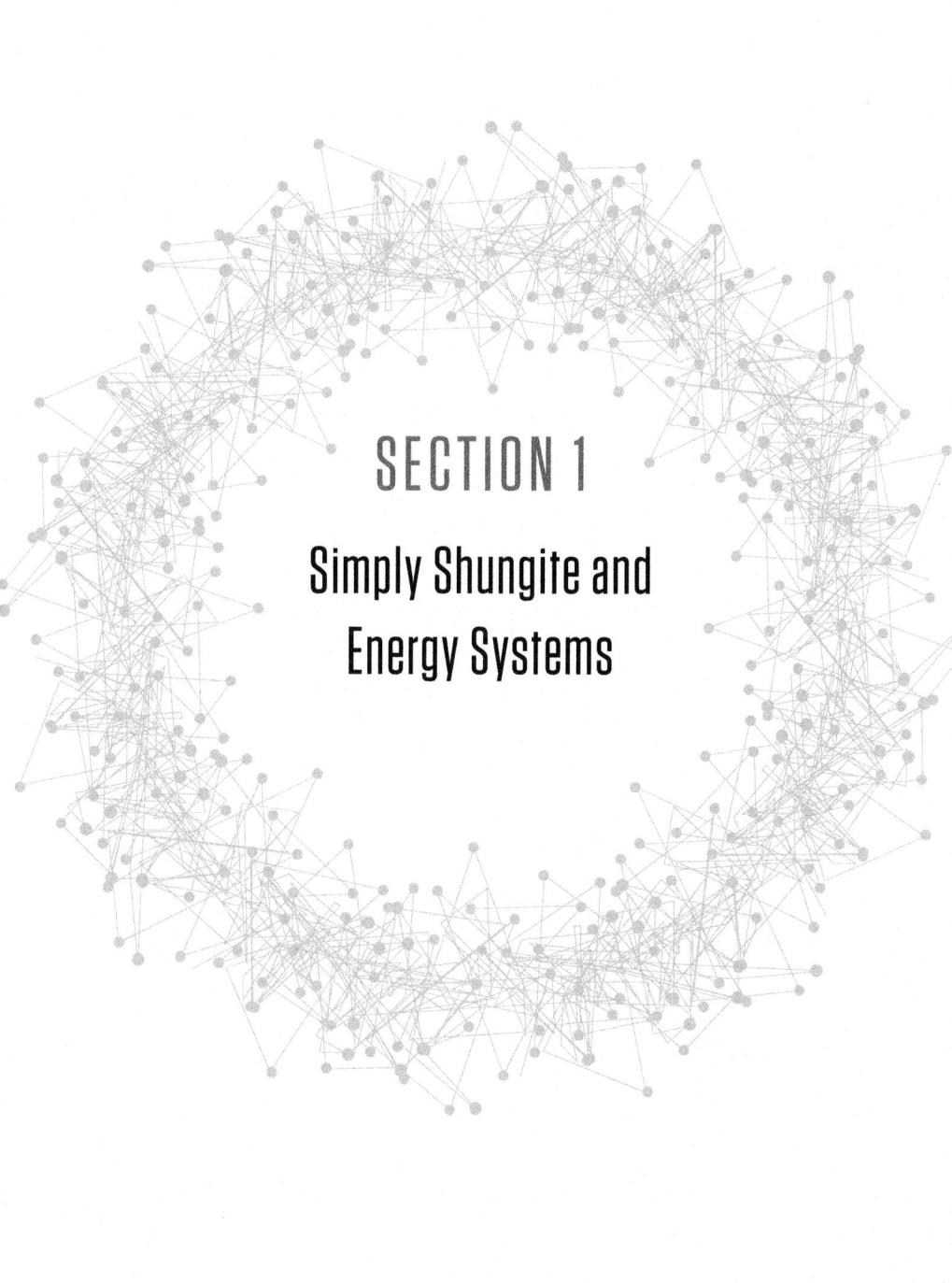

SECTION 1

Simply Shungite and Energy Systems

1

An Oraphim Exploration of Elite and Black Plain Shungite

"Shungite is something incomprehensible".
Yuri Klavdievich - Russian scientist

Shungite, the carbon-based mineraloid is the most unusual substance, it's unlike anything else on the planet, and technically not classified as a crystal which it is commonly mistaken for, and as it can not be partnered with anything else in existence even in the carbon family such as coal and diamonds who it's closest too because it broke their rules too!

Common Shungite has several variations ranging from grey to black dusty stones alongside the rarer 'Elite' stones looking more silvery and 'shiny', all of them share the same inherent properties and characteristics which are that of performing biofield enhancing, negative EMF harmonisation, absorption, air and water purification; unlike coal its closest carbon relative Shungite does not offer any resistance, allowing electrical current to flow straight through it. You can even use a flat piece to scroll your phone screen to see if it is a genuine piece, or alternatively pop a piece in the back of a torch to see it light up when the circuit is complete with the Shungite bridging the gap, unless you have voltmeters to use of course, but to see the delight on children's faces when they pop a Shungite stone in the back of a torch giving it a wobble to make the light flicker is priceless and so magical you should definitely do that once at least.

Whilst Shungite itself is not magnetic most people feel a magnetic sensation when holding any type of Shungite stones although each set of the stones often give a different feeling to the other, try it yourself by holding the stones in your finger tips and moving them very gently away from and towards each other, a slow bounce of about 4 to 6 inches apart is generally the case for most people to experience this.

Whilst the primary deposit is located near the Finnish border with Russia other locations in Brazil and Kazakhstan have also been discovered. However, these latter locations lack the certification that they contain 'fullerenes' which is the key element that is present only in the originally Finnish now Russian deposit in a place called Karelia.

The size of the Karelian deposit is still a topic of debate, some reports claim that it covers 3,475 square miles, which is approximately 5.7 times the size of Greater London, others have stated that it is only 621 square miles (two thirds the size of greater London). Regardless of its size the total reserve is estimated to be over 250 gigatons, therefore it is not about to run out any time soon debunking the myth of its scarcity. Although there are other reasons for its recent rise in price and availability, it is however thought to be more valuable than gold for its unique properties.

Shungite does not fit the established rules for geologically formed landmasses, and its origins still remain a mystery today. Despite more than a century of study by Russian and Western scientists no consensus has been reached. Various theories have been proposed, including wild theories that it is linked to a meteor, being part of the remains from the planet Phaeton, the hypothetical planet hypothesised by the Titius–Bode law to have existed between the orbits of Mars and Jupiter, the destruction of which supposedly led to the formation of the asteroid belt however this still remains unconfirmed due to anomalies which we will look at.

Shungite is mined directly from the Earth's surface as well as from one of the nine layers that make up its total depth of 400-600 feet. It is also not thought to be a lava deposit, and nothing pressed on top of it with any significant pressure during its formation. Adding to its mysterious origins Shungite contains all of the elements on the periodic table except for the radioactive ones, additionally helium3 which is typically only found in space but is found at other meteorite sites, lending a little credence to the theory of its extra-terrestrial meteoric origins; but with its unusual formation in nine layers, we must question further for a more satisfactory answer….so is that nine flat pancake like meteorites the size of a very large city? Or do we still need to keep an open mind for the true origins to still be discovered, Shungite the modern mystery.

Fullerenes which are the key to this wonderful stone's abilities have been discovered in abundance in space as seen through the Hubble telescope, but not so much here on Earth with exceptions being meteor crash sites, lightning strikes or other electrical phenomena. The meteor theory according to Professor Kovalevsky has some grounds for validity due to his microscopic photographs of Shungite showing the presence of interplanetary dust particles; the meteor would possibly date back to around 2.5 billion years ago during the 'presolar' period of the Paleoproterozoic era but this is contested as Yuri Klavdievich, Doctor of Technical Sciences, as he proposes that Shungite could have formed at the same time as our planet Earth due to the extremely high temperatures it takes to form fullerenes, he ponders "Shungite form emerged before other rocks and layers, the question is - may it be possible for Shungite to form at the same time as the planet Earth?"

The Karelia Shungite deposit contains elements from the entire periodic table suggesting that its arrival has much more to offer life than any meteorite extinction event ever documented. Further research has revealed that the earliest signs of life are located in the Karelia region near the lakes in the region Shungite is found which is nicknamed 'the belly of the Earth'.

So you see the origins of Shungite still remain a mystery to this day, and it's easy to jump to conclusions about meteors when we are asked for an opinion, but to truly know Shungite is to embrace its mystery, leaving us to wonder even more about this fascinating substance.

Free full colour picture resources available at
www.shungiteexpectmiracles.me

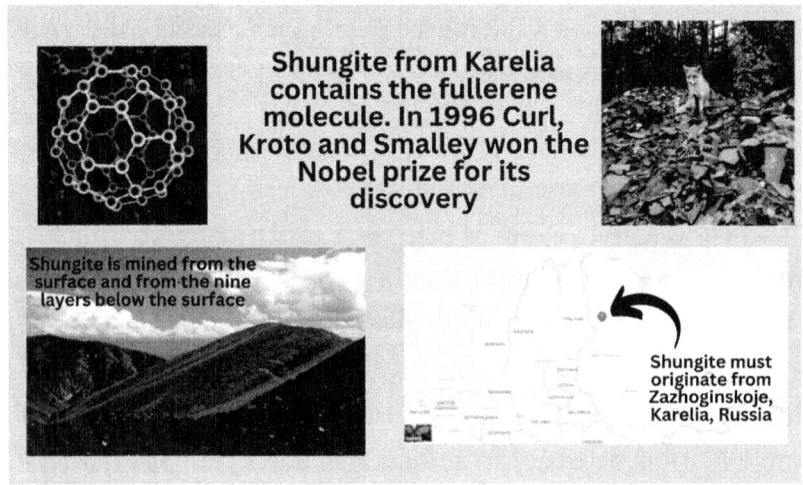

An Overview of Black Shungite

"When I put my Shungite bracelet on, it transforms my day, I am engaged, inspired, motivated and achieve what I set in motion, my lab work is transformed, with perfect results first time, how different my day is from what it was before I knew Shungite, I feel I experience my best work on these Shungite wearing days." Dr H Brew

Shungite, a rare carbon based mineral, is renowned for its healing qualities. Whilst the most expensive stones are typically believed to be the most potent, these are not always required for extraordinary results as Oraphim will share their studies of the actions of both separately. In this chapter we will examine some of the properties of black Shungite, which accounts for 99% of the total deposit and debunk some common myths about it along the way.

Properties of Black Shungite:

- It can be polished, shaped or used as rough chips, and its powder/dust is a highly effective detoxification agent with rapid results including water purification.

- Its carbon content varies between 30-64%, with darker black stones being more desirable.

- Shungite was known by the Slavs as 'Aspidian' and was believed to have remarkable water purification, healing and empowering abilities, making an army invincible against enemies.

- Shungite was also called Viper stones.

- Black Shungite was used to help a man diagnosed with two brain tumours behind his eyes. He was told he only had three months to live, with an accidental overdose of radiation therapy medication, his liver and kidney function tests were returned 'normal' with great relief and astonishing the medical staff and family. His tumours had also shrunk and he was given a life expectancy of four years.

- Smaller Shungite stones or powder are ideal, as it's best to keep a few clustered together, see it as a 'sociable' stone, as their energy joins forces to be more powerful- together rather than using one larger stone.

- Black Shungite contains naturally occurring veins of quartz and pyrite, which is associated with protection, abundance, enhancing energy and grounding energy.

- Black Shungite powder infused with pure silver particles is used by Oraphim to provide maximum EMF harmonising results which have been independently evaluated and described as 'robust protection.'

- Black Shungite is used as a natural fertiliser to increase nitrogen fixing in plants, resulting in greener leaves and larger vegetables, in studies it was proven to increase potato yields.

- Mixing Shungite powder with chicken feed can improve the health of chickens and lengthen their laying seasons.

- Shungite combined into a C60 Sea Moss jell has had excellent results in reversing the effects of what has been called 'Long C_vid'.

- Using smooth polished stones for massage is especially effective when warmed in hot water, as the Shungite emits far infrared frequencies which deeply penetrate into the body to aid the rapid repair of muscle damage, pop the warmed stones in place whilst you are sat in a chair for the evening to experience the healing they provide the following day.

- Within half an hour after Shungite rocks were submerged in water, the concentration of group D Streptococcus decreased by 10-100 times, and group A by 900 times, compared to the initial indicators. The experiment used water infused with Shungite and was pronounced to have bactericidal properties against these microorganisms. Streptococcus A which are the causative agent of angina, scarlet fever, rheumatism and group D Streptococcus (enterococci) these encompass the new genus Enterococcus comprising 13 known species and some species of streptococci which have their habitat in the intestine of animals, e.g. Streptococcus bovis, suis and equinus.

- The antibacterial action that black Shungite stones performs is easy to verify and experience for example popping small stones in the cats water bowl and the bacterial growth biofilm simply does not appear, what has been reported by some writing about Shungite is that it's unique action happens due to the fullerenes trapping the bacteria in its cage like structure and then depolarizing them causing them to become completely harmless, but this does not match with the size of the bacteria or the prevalence of the fullerenes within the stones, so there is still a mystery surrounding just exactly how Shungite is able to make clean drinkable water, yet that's exactly what it is doing for both cats and humans.

- Water infused with Shungite thus becomes not just pure drinking water, but also a molecular colloidal solution of hydrated fullerenes, which belong to a new generation of medicinal and preventive solutions with a multi-faceted effect on the body.

- One very remarkable effect that the antihistamine effect of the Shungite stones has on the body. It was found that when consumed, the level of histamine in the blood, which plays an important role in the development of most allergic diseases, decreases markedly as well as rapid recovery from diseases of the nervous system.

Diseases for the prevention and treatment of which shungite water is indicated is an ever growing list some of the more common ones are:

- anemia • various types of allergies • bronchial asthma • gastritis • dyspepsia • kidney disease • liver disease • diabetes • gallstone disease, gallbladder diseases • weakened immunity • diseases of pancreas • catarrhal disease • cardiovascular diseases • cholecystitis • chronic fatigue syndrome

Diseases that use shungite baths for prevention and treatment include:

- allergies • varicosity • dandruff, hair loss • gynecological diseases (in combination with irrigation with shungite water) • hypertension • diseases of the gastrointestinal tract: dyspepsia, gastritis, enteritis, colitis • diseases of the gallbladder • cholelithiasis • acne • diseases of the blood and lymph • urolithiasis • diseases of the genitourinary system, kidneys • neuropsychiatric diseases: depression, stress • diseases of pancreas • catarrhal disease • cardiovascular diseases • chronic fatigue syndrome, overwork

Additionally, Shungite is lipophilic with the ability to go where other antioxidants cannot go. Also other antioxidants can cause death if oversubscribed, but not Shungite. If the concentration level reaches over 10,000 times a normal dose there are absolutely no negative effects for cells. This gives everyone the opportunity to use Shungite without worry or concern; it will do its best for you and will give your body the frequency upgrade, detoxification and repair all at once without delay and its effects on our surroundings is often remarked upon.

"I've been watering my plants with water with the stones in and all of them are noticeably looking much healthier including the cactus and I've not used any plant food." Kay Nov 23

The first life assisting transformational healing Oraphim witnessed involved a gentleman Oraphim knew who was suddenly diagnosed with a brain tumour behind each eye, he was given three months to live. Oraphim gave him black Shungite stones for his drinking water and Cassie laminated a patch of powder which he wore in his hat during his next few months.

To everyone's horror he was given double the dose of radiation treatment by mistake for a short while; his liver and kidney function tests were rushed through for results to assess any damage, they were returned to everyone's surprise and joy reading completely normal. At the three month mark his treatment team said "well whatever you're doing carry on, as we are now giving you a life expectancy of four years due your improvements and due to the shrinking of the tumours", the Shungite in conjunction with the medical treatment seemed to be doing a great job.

What is interesting to note is that during recorded medical studies of radiation treatments patients' liver and kidney functions without the use of Shungite take around 2-3 months for them to return to normal levels, and with Shungite 2-3 weeks is stated. In this case they were normal *instantly*. Had Shungite risen to the challenge on this occasion and gone into overdrive to deliver a positive reading for his vital organs despite the harmful radiation treatment being doubled? What is most noteworthy is that this occurred with the use of **black** Shungite stones and not Elite Shungite which is often touted as being better and some incorrectly state that people should not bother with black Shungite!

A young man with blood clots reported that they were completely dispersed using this same black Shungite powder, he needed to rapidly detoxify as he experienced these blood clots which coincided with becoming unwell shortly after following government guidelines and agreeing to have the experimental mRN_ C_vid treatments.

A couple of friends of Oraphim's Shungite miners bought a rural dacha dwelling. They dug a well but were dismayed that the water had a foul smell of hydrogen sulphide, high colour and turbidity. Fortunately, their supplier recommended Shungite as a natural way to purify the water. They bought 50 kg of Shungite and poured it into the well; the following spring they were astonished to find that the water was crystal clear and had no odour.

After three years the water was drinkable and a sample was sent to the Pirogov laboratory, which concluded that the water only slightly exceeded the limits for iron and manganese whilst everything else was fine. It turned out that Shungite gravel was effective in cleaning the water of bacterial contaminants, nitrates and oil, and gave it active properties.

Drinking Shungite infused water has a rejuvenating effect on the body, hydrating and cleansing the skin, smoothing wrinkles, eliminating irritation, itching and rashes. Shungite water strengthens hair, giving it a healthy shine and eliminating dandruff. Moreover, this natural purifier treats various diseases such as kidney disease, liver disease, gallstone disease and heartburn as cited in many medical reports and Oraphim have received many testimonials to confirm this.

Shungite contains 108 trace minerals needed for optimum health. Its unique truncated icosahedron shape which is made up from 20 hexagons and 12 pentagons is the most stable atom available, making it an effective treatment for vegetative vascular dystonia, diseases of the gastrointestinal tract, musculoskeletal system, genitourinary system and greatly aids the circulatory system. Shungite water also relieves allergic conditions and improves the overall tone of the body.

Its reported that only 100ml of 'Shungite' water each day is a medically measured dose that is highly effective, simply use a few stones to activate the water which can be left for a maximum efficacy of three days to infuse with healing fullerenes as this way it also creates the tastiest water too, but you can drink it straight away and it will still be highly effective, purified and healing.

All animals love Shungite water, adding three tiny stones to a cat's water bowl for example, stops the bacterial biofilm forming on top. Adding Shungite to a fish tank had remarkable results in the successful reproduction rates for the fish populating the tank, alongside another fish owner touting his fish to be the biggest specimens ever seen to grow by the owner!

An Overview of Elite Stones

Elite stones are a rarer and highly sought after variety of Shungite, constituting a mere 1% of the Karelian deposit. They are a harder stone which is extremely light in weight for their size and when you hold them they are less dusty than regular Shungite stones; although they can be very brittle and prone to breakage making them generally not suitable for turning into shaped bowls, cups or beads. The layers visible in the makeup of the Elite stones suggest that they were once molten liquid that slowly cooled over a very long time resulting in veins that span 18 inches throughout the deposit. This process is also known as annealing, which is also utilised in the manufacture of rare earth magnets.

These stones are excavated by hand and they are found only in veins that are 40 cm wide and elite stones are composed of 98% carbon; sometimes with ochre coloured 'rust' deposits which are oxidised Pyrite which is a basic compound of sulphate called Jarosite which is completely harmless.

Oraphim adds Elite Shungite powder to their pendants and pyramids to produce an even 'lighter and higher' frequency. Other producers, such as Richard Winters at The Vortex, have also noted the transformational healing properties of Elite Shungite when combined with other crystals for various desired effects and wellbeing.

Despite the claims made by some shops and vendors that Elite Shungite is more effective owing to its higher carbon content, research has demonstrated that black Shungite (grade 2) is superior for electromagnetic devices. The magneto-resistance ratio (MR) in black Shungite $C60$ is around one order of magnitude larger than that of Elite $C70$ based devices at room temperature. This makes black Shungite a better material for use in negative man-made EMF harmonising solutions which confirms the same assertion made by Nancy L Hopkins on this topic.

When it comes to water purification, healing and detoxing it's not necessary to purchase the most expensive Elite Shungite stones. Any 'black' grade of Shungite stone will do the job effectively. Don't be fooled by the idea that Elite Shungite stones are better than their cheaper counterparts; when it comes to purifying water they only work quicker to do the same job by a few seconds and the Oraphim Silver Activated toggles had the fasted chlorine nullifying effects of all.

Oraphim's water analysis results demonstrate that even a pinch of common black Shungite is better than a 15 stage filter. If you do feel a greater connection to one type of Shungite over another, trust your instincts and follow Shungite's calling as both black and Elite Shungite stones are beneficial and you will be providing yourself with great stones either way.

In summary all grades of Shungite stones can be effective for personal development as they are energetically enhancing, and they are all integrated parts of the whole quantum fabric that is spread all over the world, match them up with your own body's quantum magnetic energy field for a powerful transformation and gently glide your way into a new frequency!

It's hard to believe that one material could be so effective in every natural form it's found in, even in its smallest quantities such as a pinch of its powder. We are naturally hesitant to settle for anything less than the best and often think more is needed, but black Shungite should never be regarded as second best, it has astounding efficacy, working seamlessly in tandem to surpass all conventional standards of effectiveness. In fact, you may even notice tangible results within a remarkably short period of time yourself.

Energising Your water for Healing and Purifying Your Water for Drinking

No Need to Replace Shungite Stones 100% Natural and 100% Safe

- Healing Fullerenes C60
- Heavy Metal Removal/Detoxification
- Powerful Antioxidant
- Greater Hydration
- Structured Water
- Rinse and reuse stones without the need to replace them.

2

Harmonising Harmful Frequencies

"Shungite is a stone of apparent contradictions, holding the tension of several opposites." Yuri Klavdievich Doctor of Technical Sciences also asserts that Shungite could have been formed at the beginning of the Universe or even before this because it is so unique, thus making it a 'genesis' stone and a modern mystery at the same time.

Shungite is a powerful tool that aligns all vibrations with nature and elevates your body's energy frequencies. Many people have described feeling a 'whoosh' sensation when they first wear Shungite, indicating that their frequency has been lifted to new heights.

The latest release of 5G - 60 GHz - is a cause for concern as it is considered a 'weapons grade Wi-Fi' frequency by Wi-Fi weapons experts Nancy L Hopkins and Mark Steele among other outspoken academics and critics. The damaging effects include the fact that it can heat up the body's water molecules, create cortisol hormone release and negativity affect arterial blood oxygenation and subtle heart rate variability. Fortunately silver activated Shungite can positively alter the magnetic field and reverse and alter the harmful man-made square wave, preventing 'Necrosis' or overheating of the body's cells as well as latest studies from the National Institute of Health publishing evidence that is calms the whole physical system from 'Wi-Fi' and mobile phones negative side effects.

Nancy L Hopkins is the discoverer and subsequent developer of the silver-infused enhancing technique that has made Shungite a truly effective EMF harmonising solution, with its ability to work even more rapidly as a healing solution in many situations too. This discovery was made by accident when the nuggets she was wrapping with silver wire absorbed the silver and she recognised this was an important breakthrough. She then began to examine the phenomenon on a molecular level and with the aid of Walt Silva who helped to test the effects and devise production methods, led to the launch of silver-infused Shungite through her platform 'Cosmic Reality.'

Hopkins is a pioneer in many areas having been the first female to head up a US military department. Her extensive knowledge of Russia and electromagnetic systems led her to conceive of the idea of Wi-Fi warfare applications back in the 1960s. Her vast and unusual experiences go far beyond many peoples day to day lives, covering a wide area of metaphysical and extra-terrestrial concepts and experiences which she has detailed in her book titled 'Cosmic Reality.' Her latest publication 'Shungite Reality: A Study of Energy,' is full of fascinating facts, metaphysical wisdom and even a testimonial mention for Oraphim on page 111.

Having experts such as Hopkins discussing the issues around the dangers of Wi-Fi and its development to fifth generation telecommunications is vital to the conversation to help many more people see that there is much at stake for our health and future generations.

The White House Press Briefing stated on the 12th March 2020, titled 'President Donald J Trump Is Committed to Safeguarding America's Vital Communications Networks and Securing 5G Technology,' highlights the significance of ensuring that the country's communication networks are **safe**, secure and reliable and this legislation signed by President Trump is to protect these networks from foreign adversaries. This is especially important, given the link between 5G technology and C_vid-19 symptoms as was published in a study by the National Institutes of Health.

The subsequent Executive Order on the 1st May 2020 regarding 'Bulk Power Systems', which included the UK in making subverted technologies 'safe,' is outlined in H.R.4998 – Secure and Trusted Communications Networks Act of 2019. The British government's decision to replace Huawei and its 5G network in the UK is possibly a notable response to this issue, in conjunction with not wanting the overseeing eye of a Chinese National 'spying' on the nation's telecommunications as outlined by MP Ian Duncan-Smith; but what about our nation's physical safety, and why was Prime Minister Teresa May brought in for questioning over the matter by the police? There is still much to be researched on the topic.

What would be the mainstream solution to making the 5G network safe?

The answer can be found in what are called 'Harmonising shunts,' which use soft magnetic alloys made of cobalt, vanadium and iron as this compound 'attenuates' 5 G frequencies, this reversal of the harmful signals of 5G telecommunications were detailed in the Institute of Electrical and Electronics Engineers conference paper on mitigating the harm caused by 5G.

Interestingly, they are also known by their periodic table abbreviations Co (cobalt) V (vanadium) Fe x2 (iron), COVFEFE - a term that gained widespread attention after being tweeted by President Donald Trump mistaking his tweeting about 'coffee' to many a misplaced hilarity. Silver activated Shungite is mimicking the action of these harmonising filters so that the frequencies are attenuated and are no longer harmful waves, silver activated Shungite is a valuable tool in protecting against modern damaging technologies.

While it is somewhat encouraging to report on these Executive Orders that are focused on beneficial protective orders from a governmental body, further proof is still being actively sought, with the asking for signs of proof that these systems harms to have been nullified with a safe alternative to have actually been put in place.

It seems like an invisible war is being waged and we are all a part of it whether we like it or not. We need help to protect ourselves from an extinction level threat on many fronts as 5G decimates the insect life in the ground as well as the bees flying around; we must individually seek ways to create a positive reality and develop strategies and solutions for keeping well. Shungite can work on many different levels -physically as well as to help amplify your heart's positive intentions, making your wishes a significant part of the new frequency that is transforming the world for the better.

Protecting children has naturally been paramount in the mind of loving parents throughout time and invisible, invading, modern toxins created by technology adds to parental burdens; an unavoidable threat literally right in front of our eyes as we stare at screens with consequences we still don't fully comprehend. Consider the little known fact that babies' eyes are still developing up until the age of two and LCD screens can cause permanent damage to their developing eyes, yet screens are now the modern babysitter and how we communicate over vast distances to connect to our loved ones in our modern separated world.

Despite the increasing evidence of the health implications of man-made 'smart waves', including myelin sheath degeneration leading to conditions such as Chronic Fatigue Syndrome (CFS), Myalgic Encephalitis (ME), Multiple Sclerosis (MS) and 'Cyber Sickness', the dangers of modern technology and Wi-Fi are still either an unknown danger or fairly low concern for many, alongside considering the cost of living crisis that has been creeping up on families alike for many lifetimes, culminating in the engineered modern cash crisis crescendo we find ourselves in late 2023, the Oraphim team were inspired to work with Shungite to bring affordable solutions to you. As the utilisation of mobile technology continues to expand, and is unlikely to recede any time soon, we need to adopt solutions that are effective, affordable and simple and do not need replacing.

Shungite now has many scientific and medical studies that back up its efficacy, which is generally not the case with other stones and crystals to the extent that Shungite has, and this puts Shungite in a class of its own. Cassie and Rich's research was turning up astounding transformations and their educational enthusiasm to share this with others was starting to kick in! They discovered that Shungite has surprising physical sensations too, that can often be felt like repelling and attracting magnets, even tingling in areas of the body where problems occurred, they were hooked and there was no stopping its emergence into the UK with their passion, creativity and drive.

They were in a unique position to develop their products due to being accepted to help guests at a Retreat Centre, this meant that their accommodation was covered by volunteering at the centre. For these two years they were working part-time care jobs, giving them time to be able to develop their range of Shungite products. Then they moved to a quiet rural trailer/caravan park to keep their overheads low, giving Shungite their undivided attention, they progressed to be able to launch 'Oraphim Ltd'.

One of Shungite's more popular uses is to enhance and purify tap water making it taste much better and clearing it of chemicals and impurities; but its benefits go far beyond that. Shungite has shown to be effective in treating a wide range of conditions, including under-active thyroid, heart palpitations, multiple skin conditions, arthritis, Fibromyalgia, MS and ME symptoms and even stories of it positively affecting cancer - miraculously.

So how can one stone do all these things?

Shungite is a quantum adaptogen, meaning it works in a unique way with each individual. It can produce a particle-like beam that can target and support struggling organs, single out damaged cells for repair or rejuvenate damaged nervous systems often caused by man-made electrical signals, poisons or toxins; it can also balance the mineral content of each cell in the body as well as identifying toxins for removal or nullification. Shungite energy operates in ways beyond our imaginations by interacting with unseen quantum networks, connecting you with its source in ancient Karelia; your new knowledge on the topic of Shungite will embed you with new appreciation for your integral role in the creation of how you positively affect the world around you, just by being a great you, and there's so much more to share with you on an even deeper level.

The combination of Oraphim and Shungite has resulted in a one-stop-shop for those seeking a truly unique and effective Shungite experience. With its rapid effects and remarkable benefits, it's no wonder that people are turning to Oraphim for their health, wellness and transformational needs.

Described by Lisa Renee 'Oraphim' is believed to be closely linked to the 'Elohim' and embodies the elemental frequencies, which she outlines are a blueprint for humanity that has the power to transmute itself across the dimensionalised time matrix. The Oraphim name refers to the founder races and Rich was instrumental in recognising that Shungite is active in accessing and even enhancing humanities blueprint instrumental in unlocking new information locked in the DNA, with scientific discoveries and ancient mythical legends regarding Shungite's properties matching, this is the 'genesis' stone that created an environment for our souls to inhabit this planet right here, you are the 'missing link' to instigating the next phase of human evolution and Shungite is the key to unlocking an amazing future for us in many including technological advances.

Shungite is a remarkable find much like the person using it, whilst people describe its energy affecting isolated parts of their body, providing rapid relief and repair where needed, even going as far as exclaiming that their wings have opened, what will you feel, or experience when you interact with this fascinating mineraloid?.

What makes Shungite so effective is its interactive nature with each of us. It is highly responsive to our energy systems; Shungite being an adaptogen is working on the whole field as well as isolating a particular part where it's energy is needed, this is also known as a quantum healing or scalar energy healing modality, essentially it 'scans' each person's unique EMF field then gets to work unblocking, repairing and raising their vibration which is then putting them into a new state of higher frequencies in a calm and balanced way. This can lead to some individuals experiencing a burst of energy, whilst others may be surprised to find a deep and restful sleep due to the balancing nature of its effects which exceeded their expectations.

This interaction with our energy systems is providing feedback to the quantum field which is then sending the correct frequency to tune you physically and with powerful energy system upgrades, its ability to deliver the perfect biofeedback solution on many levels both biologically on a mineral balancing level as well as energetically accessing your potential is a rare and unique effect. This energy interaction can be sent as a wave and as a particle beam, with energy pulsed at intervals to unblock specific energy blockages in the human physical body / energy system or neural pathways.

Shungite's efficacy is beyond dispute, it is also always changing and expanding as you will learn more about later. Some have even observed white or gold lines that have appeared on the stones during their own transformation that were not there before, the stones can even surprisingly break into smaller pieces whilst holding them, this multiplication of Shungite is delivering even more power which is providing a even greater potential for healing and growth with each use, Shungite becomes more powerful the smaller it gets which is opposite to the way crystals are taught to work.

A mother of five shared her story of how, during a chaotic family moment, to her surprise her Shungite stone broke into many pieces whilst she held it in her hands. Her friends suggested that it would no longer work and that she should give up on it and get a new one; Cassie comforted her and explained that the stone's breaking into many pieces actually makes it more effective, leading her to have a new-found appreciation for the power of Shungite.

Cassie can recall a gentleman's feedback on how he no longer had to dust his TV as often, as the Shungite stone changed the static energy created by the TV, making it less attractive to dust, leading to a deeper understanding of the changes it has for all electrical fields mechanical and biological, simply benefiting us in many ways including allowing yourself to separate from old paradigms and develop a lighter step moving forward, energetically speaking its changing how we attract experiences in our lives too, less dusting required as we are cleansed by Shungite and held in a new frequency.

During the development phase Cassie became aware that she could actually feel the energetic shifts that were occurring as people played with the stones, and she is witness to the transformation in people from a state of slight chaotic panic or anxiety to gentle peaceful receptivity, which mostly only takes their first few days of being with Shungite.

There have been many extraordinary experiences reported and there are some to get inspired by at the back of this book, but to share a couple now would be nice, a lady who had suffered from Chronic Fatigue for 24 years, upon purchasing an Oraphim pyramid, her energy was fully restored the very next morning, she returned to the event to express her joy with tears streaming down her face. Another gentleman was pleasantly surprised that his arthritis had eased considerably overnight after being around his brand new Oraphim made pyramid. Could these Oraphim pyramids really be transforming lives over night?

As you embark on your journey through this book you'll gain scientific insights and simple, inspirational ideas to help you use this life changing resource. The more you understand the topic in a new way, the more you'll appreciate how special it is. For you to have come across it right now- it's a gift from the heavens connecting you with the creation of our planet and you may even be holding some of this rare resource as you read this today.

3

The Positive Side of Electromagnetic Fields

It's important to recognise that EMFs have both positive and negative aspects. As you grow and develop your own human bioenergy field changes and develops. Shungite is a powerful tool that tunes your frequency and enhances your energy field, allowing for greater positive experiences to be attracted to you or alternatively it can be seen as for you to be in tune with receiving your hearts desires; this leads very quickly to developing appropriate interactions with others that honour your boundaries as well as honouring others sensitivities and with a bonus of better health all round.

Enhancing human electo-magnetic fields has many people even reporting feeling as though their wings are opening up and their heads have a gentle whoosh of new energy they have never experienced before, these are all effects from changes in the energy field created by each human heart beat and these frequencies are emitted far beyond the physical body, Shungite is simply making these fields stronger and bigger.

Understanding the positivity associated with EMFs is crucial before analysing man-made artificial electromagnetic fields such as those emitted by household devices and mobile phones. It's essential to know that all living beings create an electrical 'field' that surrounds them. This field connects us to our environment, holds our memories and emotions, and links us to our past, present and future. Interestingly, the human eye technically has the ability to see these coloured fields but most adults have lost this art. Children often still have this ability but it is filtered out as they grow older.

According to Kevin Doe and Susie Sykes, agree with the insights published in the rare and important book 'SuperNature' by Lyall Watson, the energy field surrounding living beings are highly visible still to babies; a genuine smile from the heart can expand one's aura in colour, density and form. When interacting with a young child you may notice that they smile instinctively and gaze at your head and upper torso. This is because they can resonate with the vibrant energy of love and see colours such as yellows, golds and greens. You can even calm an upset child in a store by smiling at them with a compassionate aura.

If you ask a young child about what colours they can see around people, or your child has started to talk about seeing colours around people, consider taking them to a Mind Body Soul event with an aura photographer, before showing them any imagery, ask them what colours surround your body and then have your image taken - the results may surprise you.

Cassie has had her aura photographed many times over 25 years and has discovered that it evolves alongside personal development. As she transformed, her aura morphed too, the separation of white and orange light balls in her field in her late teens merging into a solid mass of colours. It's as if she was connecting the dots of her own energy field!

Physically we seem so separate to each other yet our energy fields overlap, infuse, affect and inspire each other; our thoughts live outside of our bodies and can get picked up by others, we can think of a distant friend or relative and they phone us out of the blue or walk round the corner towards us. Each and every one of us are connected in a quantum network we often call 'coincidence' and it's this network connection that Shungite is strengthening, but is there more to it than that, how do we develop in a way that shapes us for the better?

Cassie had an epiphany one day when her young son made a statement that changed her perspective on death and also started the ball rolling the mechanics of 'thoughts' existing beyond one's brain. Pointing to her belly he declared, "I remember before I was in there." This caught Cassie off guard as she had never much considered the idea of a 'before life.' Although stories of reincarnation exist she never expected such profound insights from her own child. It was as though her own thoughts and emotions had manifested in her surroundings and were picked up by him and being answered by his experiences; she had wanted and needed some kind of reassurance as her own fears were looming about death, it was as if her thoughts were outside of her body and not contained within her head.

In today's digital age we can easily access information on any topic, from 'past life regression' to 'near death experiences' with just a few clicks. However, this wasn't the case over two decades ago when Cassie considered her son's words. She had been 'putting it out there' by simply thinking, what we think is potent and powerful. Each of us has a naturally inquisitive mind that is forever foraging for answers but without the understanding that we also inhibit space outside of the physical barriers of our skull and skin we are continually surprised when the world delivers the exact reply, has this inspired the worship of the worldly matter instead of a creator of the world?

The message being shared here is that each of us holds the key to unlocking many gifts and knowledge; we are able to activate the answers we need, revealing many truths that have been purposefully hidden until now. By simply enhancing your energy field's strength with Shungite you can access and affect your surroundings by being the best you; in an empowered way it's vitally important to continue questioning and creating the opportunities for the answers to show up in your life, and a little comment, or a passing thought can create a life changing frequency shift - which is all it takes sometimes to change our lives.

Your human body with its electromagnetic field creates a quantum bubble around it, this is also known as a torus field, which is often being depleted, but by having it enhanced with powerful silver activated Shungite there are many more experiences and multidimensional connections awaiting you, and there are many exciting experiences just waiting to align with your vibration.

Physical and frequency experiences can be enhanced with Shungite simply in your pocket; the more you question the more you are learning how to tap into quantum fields around you, it's as simple as 'ask and it shall be given.'

Appreciating that it is your inquisitive mind that is taking this step in discovering the wonders of life, and you have decided to develop in knowledge by picking up this book because you want to have answers about a stone called Shungite, answers from questions, firstly we have to create the questions as we go along. You are learning about Shungite and yourself at the same time; but will Shungite and yourself be more magical and mysterious the more you learn about them?

From the first 'Adam' who ate the apple to each atom in our bodies having its own energy field, just as it is represented in the apple, this field is also known as your torus energy field around your body; the allegory of the apple is a mirror of the body and every cell in it.

Our bioelectromagnetic field, also known as the aura, is essential in connecting us to our environment which is creating a feedback loop of our own thoughts and desires, a conduit for energy connecting us with the Earth and beyond. By working with Shungite it naturally enhances the loving and beneficial frequencies that pair us more strongly with our natural world, and we become more integrated and less harmed by man-made signals.

The enhancing effect Shungite has on us is remarkable due to its ability to create a stronger and expanded torus field, experienced as a stronger quantum energy bubble around us which is intrinsically linked to space and time, you are no longer 'depressed' by external forces in the same way as before. This time bubble aligns opportunities and is instrumental in our ability to move us to becoming the observer in our situations instead of reactionary or emotionally 'triggered' as easily. Instead of being on the back-foot there's even the ability to perceive new possibilities in many situations; by integrating with these new positive choices and creating experiences from a higher perspective allows us to respond much better and with a new ability to take responsibility for your responses whatever the situation. With these more appropriate responses we can safely instil boundaries that may have slipped or not have been developed properly in the first place and these do need enforcing appropriately at times; also to be experienced is the beautiful balance as the gentle silence envelops you and allows a new ability of realising that we can keep our thoughts as just that, a 'thought' which can also be a relief from conflict and ongoing negative perceptions which can cause depression.

You may see that with these new emotional coping abilities we gain a greater appreciation for ourselves and others within the intricate workings of each busy day, and the many souls all going about their daily lives around us. It becomes much easier to interact with people, your appreciation may turn to gratitude for how it all matches up at the end of each day and even see it as a marvellous miracle and see your part in it for others to experience something wonderful too.

With Shungite we can easily ease ourselves out of old paradigms of personal negative reactions or worries, with the calming reflections from the quantum field becoming a new normal, a new trusting and joy which we have been seeking is often attained and its transformation occurs relatively quickly. Consider your current situation and ask yourself how you would wish it to be different for others around you; what does this new wished for state *feel* like and what does it look like for *them*?

How can we be sure Shungite can help us and provide artificial electromagnetic harmonisation; and how can we tell if there is a difference in us and our appliances? This is what we will turn our attention to next.

Whilst EMF radiation meters are commonly used to measure a device's harmful magnetic electrical energy output levels they have their limitations, for example they do not detect living energy fields as this is a subtle energy not in its range, they also do not detect the direction which the energies spins which is a key factor in its ability to be harmful or healthy. This is why we need to look at a range of different measuring methods which have been explored by others and also what is available for people to try for themselves.

Kirlian photography has revealed many times the astonishing and often unseen energetic energy surrounding many things including that of the energy emitted from Shungite stones which create a stronger 'tentacle' of energy when clustered together, this is not picked up or read by EMF meters but has been captured by Professor Sofia Blank and it's her images that show how this is multiplied when there is a cluster of stones together.

This amazing Kirlian technology is able to show us the blueprints of living information. For example when the aura of a leaf with part of it cut away is captured, the entire leaf's outline is visible on the photograph. The blueprint for the whole leaf is there and that is the same for us even when we are missing a part of the physical body.

To capture the transformation that silver activated Shungite can bring to you Oraphim enlisted the help of Laura and Kevin Doe at Aura-interpretations, an aura expert and Laura, our willing participant, a test subject who had never held Shungite before. Kevin photographed her using his traditional Kirlian photography set-up, which was produced by Guy Coggins using the analogue Fuji film, this revealed her electromagnetic signature on the polaroid film; this technology was originally developed in Russia. The difference between the two photographs was astounding, with Laura's aura changing completely from green to yellow-orange. The experience even resulted in sensations of transformation in her Throat Chakra.

Everyone has unique aura colours and there is no negative or better colour than any other persons. However, experiencing a difference in frequency can highlight different personal attributes of your personal character and skill sets.

This was one of the first Shungite transformation techniques that visibly showed the difference Shungite makes that Oraphim were instrumental in bringing to the growing body of evidence that Shungite really does change lives!

The human body's resonance aura field, which is also its blueprint, can be tapped into to relieve discomfort. For instance, the energy field of a person with a missing limb may retain memories of the accident that caused its loss. By clearing the morphogenic resonance field, which includes the place, time and space of the accident's occurrence is beneficial, as this can be a cause of reoccurring stress upon the body. Using Shungite pyramids can be an extremely effective way to release these morphogenic disturbances held in the energy field and in turn alleviating and releasing stress, pain and anxiety from the physical body.

The impact of past experiences on our physical and emotional wellbeing must not be overlooked, these experiences can be stored in our memory and energy layers, which are beyond our physical skin, leading to depression, negative responses and harmful behaviour. Even the recollection of the birthing process can cause distress in children and their parents each birthday as its approaches on the calendar.

Each year as we pass through the time of a stressful event, our body recreates the tension and anxiety associated with it; we can be locked into the quantum relationship with place, space, event and ourselves. Releasing yourself from past experiences can be most beneficial for breaking negative responses.

We can help ourselves greatly by learning to step aside and embody the observer role, which is key to achieving the creation of new desires, directions in life and shedding old ways, which is easier with a quantum energy entering our energy field and this is one way Shungite helps.

In the pyramids and magnet sections of this book, you will learn simple techniques to dispel negative energy and transform your wellbeing, with easy techniques to aid the frequencies of your family and friends in fun and interactive ways with a whole host of exhilarating sensations to be experienced at the same time.

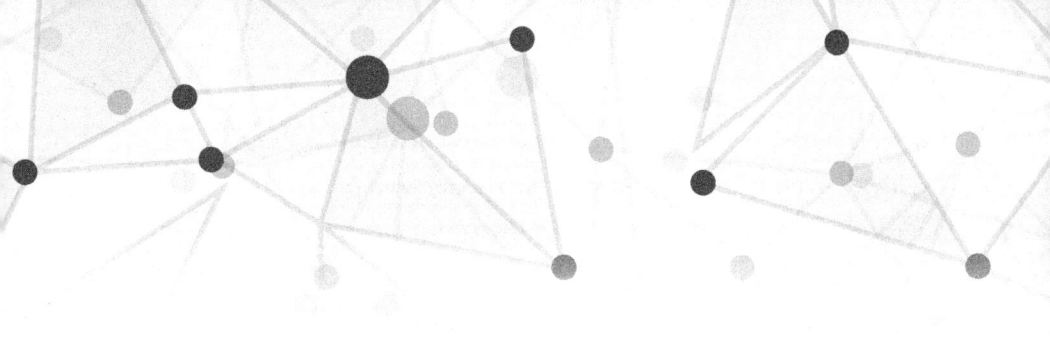

4

The Significance of 'Waves'

"People should think things out fresh and not just accept conventional terms and the conventional way of doing things."
R Buckminster Fuller

Electromagnetic 'Waves' come in various forms, each with its own set of frequencies, much like brain waves that range from waking to sleeping to coma. Shungite infuses you with new, higher frequencies to ones you've already been used to experiencing which you may never have even considered as an 'experience' before, with Silver Activated Shungite taking it up a significant notch higher.

Ideally through our daily journey each of us should experience a full spectrum of brain waves, without each vital one of these brain states we will start to encounter problems, and when we run into issues the pharmaceutical industry has a cocktail of chemicals readily available at the first sign of trouble. By looking to naturally balance our frequencies and brain states we can support a healthy and balanced lifestyle without added side effects from chemicals; otherwise we are destined to continue our descent into decay with prescribed medicines causing many more problems and harmful side effects that we had not bargained for in the process. So how can a simple Shungite stone help us and neutralise the effects of harmful man-made devices?

For centuries electrical power has played a crucial role in human civilisation. The commonly taught belief is that Benjamin Franklin discovered electricity in 1752 by observing lightning strikes and realising that this could generate power. However, it wasn't until fairly recently that electricity became widely accessible to the general population in the developed world; with many in the Third World still waiting for the 'flick of the switch' for them to join the 'developed world'.

By design or chance, we may never know, it was decided to spin the generated electrons that we call electricity in the opposite direction to nature, which is entropic and degrading. For the past 270 years humanity has been using this entropic electrical 'sine wave' to power our homes and devices.

Nikolai Aleksandrovich Kozyrev's experiments showed that energy and frequency movement has either a left hand or right hand spin direction, with the left hand being 'entropic' and degrading, whilst the right hand is expansive, enhancing and energy-giving with a much slower decay rate.

More recently the invention of 'smart' technologies which are a completely different generation of 'square' waves, developed for faster than needed two way telecommunications comes as new causes for concern because to put it simply, 5G is problematic because squares are not found in nature.

There are increasing numbers of cases where people are experiencing unpleasant burning sensations, and are even unable to use modern technology at all. With birth defects attributed to mobile phones being kept near the unborn child, we have the potential to harm the next generations without even knowing it. The term 'smart' is in fact an abbreviation for 'Self-Monitoring Analysis and Reporting Technology', although it is claimed that it is used with its meaning of 'clever' to describe any kind of available technology that allows users to connect with internet networks. Is it actually listening, 'google' can hear your questions and fetch up trivia in a split second when help is needed, but who could it possibly be reporting to beyond that and why?

We can actually look deeply within for answers as we contemplate the fact that each cell in the body emits light which gets distorted and becomes incoherent by man-made electromagnetic fields. Oraphim's silver activated Shungite corrects this issue by putting each cell's light back into a coherent state, allowing us to shine and assimilate new frequencies on a cellular level. This was confirmed by the independent autonomic response testing with the use of the Polfilter photon light meter. By measuring the light photons as each leaves the nervous system and oscillates, each cell's light aligns with the metal bars this then lights up the Polfilter apparatus, whereas the damaged field sends out a scattered array of light photons, which shows incoherence and indicates 'blocked regulation' which in turn also highlights the negative impact on the organs functions too.

To maintain overall health it's crucial to take breaks from screens including social media interactions which cause emotional triggers leading to hormonal imbalances and leads to affected energy centres and organs in the body, with the addictive dopamine responses being met through technology and not by healthy kind human contact and interactions; as we still react energetically if not physically, and biochemical reactions from stress affects us internally even on these subtle levels, every reaction creates energy that has to find its resting place within- if it is not processed, released and grounded.

Achieving this vital balance in our lives is essential, and immersing ourselves in nature by spending time in parks and the countryside can help achieve it. This provides an opportunity to breathe in cleaner air, stretch our legs, gaze over long distances and walk barefoot. This allows our body to ground through ion exchange, which releases inflammation held in the body and importantly allows for the excess energy our body is holding on to - to simply let go; as with each beat of your heart your body creates electrical energy which needs discharging. It's entirely possible that we are the 'free energy devices' that are powering our world in more ways than you may have considered before.

Non-ionizing radiation (NIR) refers to electromagnetic radiation from our plugged in world, hand held devices, including phones that seemingly emit these, which do not have sufficient energy to ionise (remove electrons from) atoms or molecules; instead this energy is converted to heat, and depending on a person's exposure time and the energy concentration of the radiation, it can have a range of damaging effects, including the heating of the head and hands while using a mobile phone for example, and this is why it can lead to burns in extreme cases and is much more damaging the younger the user.

Measuring artificial energy created by household devices can be a very eye opening and an alarming exercise, with extremely high readings coming from all sockets and cables trailing everywhere.

When using EMF meters some fluctuations with regard to space and time can result in 'hot spots' which are highly localised amplifications inside your building due to high frequency waves being reflected or absorbed. These hot spots can change places during the day or season, and even metal furniture or salt lamps can emit extremely high readings, causing concern for those assessing their radiation exposure.

Green Aura   Aura 1 hour later   **Orange Aura**

Frequency differences are measurable with Kirlian adapted cameras:

Oraphim and Kevin Doe (Aura-interpretations) Before and *with* a silver activated Shungite pendant made by Oraphim

The human eye is able to see much more than the limited narrow band of visible frequencies that surround us.
(if encouraged/acknowledge to at an early age)

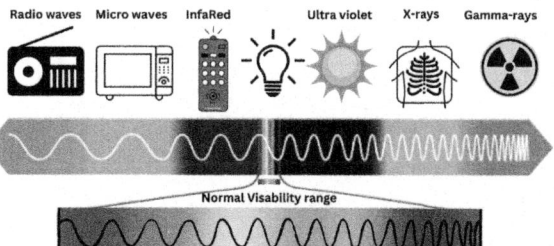

Veda Austin's water freezing technique (hydraglyphs) showing 'waves' which the Shungite energy has imprinted the water with, these are Aether Perturbations, these also match the mycelium, and scalar Energy hydroglyphs, Shungite is communicating the network that Shungite creates

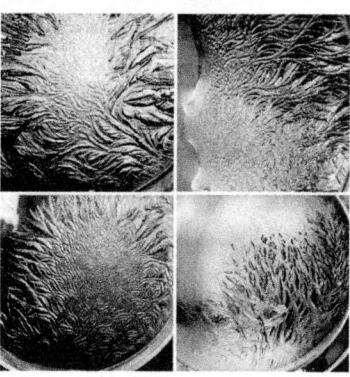

This illustration depicts the range of mechanical frequencies we encounter, starting with the lowest non-ionizing radiation frequencies such as radio waves right up to more damaging and even fatal radioactive frequencies, and that very small rainbow section in the centre is the little portion that we can see, alongside the electromagnetic frequencies that our bodies create which can not be detected by EMF meters, the hydro glyphs captured Veda Austin show the ripples in the aether created by vibration energy emissions from Shungite stones.

Shungite is a powerful mineraloid that can prevent necrosis or overheating of the body's cells. This happens because man-made electromagnetic waves spin in the opposite direction to human biofrequency 'waves' which was discovered by Nikolai Kozyrev. However silver activated Shungite can harmonise these frequencies to a much greater degree with *permanent effect* and create an environment more aligned with nature. By doing so it can also smooth out and rectify the harmful Wi-Fi 'square' wave to a natural sine wave much more effectively, which is in line with nature's design, giving relief from negative non-ionizing radiation and protection from your many plugged in devices including mobile phones. The result is that the plain Shungite stones often have to 'reset' causing for example a video call to need to reconnect several times during a 2 hour period, but the silver activated Oraphim Shungite sticker when applied will harmonise the frequencies once and for all and not need to reset the frequencies after that.

Oraphim often take the time to educate people in knowing what protection the different forms of Shungite can give, as it's vitally important to comprehend the limitations of just placing Shungite stones around your 'smart' technology or on your phone in comparison to the comprehensive job silver activated Shungite solutions provide for the health of your vital organs and overall wellbeing as well as the smooth uninterrupted working of your technology.

Rainer Schneiders' work examined the impact of electromagnetic fields (EMF) on heart rate variability (HRV), saliva cortisol, arterial blood oxygenation, and tympanic ear-drum membrane temperature, with his results from studying the potential effects of Shungite to counter EMF induced stress the conclusions that Rainer published in the NIH National Library of Medicine proved beyond a shadow of a doubt that using Shungite dramatically reduced the effects of the harmful mobile phones. He was further surprised that Shungite when used in a double blind study had an even greater effect, when the participant did not know they were using Shungite their cortisol levels plummeted even lower then when they picked up the phones! Which is stunning as this is the basis for the work that Oraphim do, whilst many EMF solutions are aesthetically plain Oraphim believe that your gift of a beautiful Shungite item with their unique artistic finishes are just the key to helping in a quiet and unannounced way, inspired by Robert Buckminsterfuller who stated *"if the solution is not beautiful, I know it is wrong."*

Shungite acts as an antihistamine, helping repair the myelin sheath that covers our nerves axons and it's these vital inner biological systems which are constantly absorbing and being damaged by all man-made electromagnetic frequencies.

Our physical systems are integrated and layered over each other and we often don't give them much thought; buried deep entwined around our skeletal system is our information superhighway- the nerves, interdependently operating together are our organs, with the water we drink flowing in to and around every cell, little known crowd surfing hydrogen cells keep us searching for connections and beyond these- our perceptions - all keeping us here on planet Earth, you are an essential soul in our big wide world, how we feel about ourselves becomes reflected in our environment too, and this is often influenced by the unhealthy systems in place around us. Small changes we make can have an enormous ripple effect on others around us, thus a tiny piece of Shungite firstly alters you positively which creates a wave of change through others.

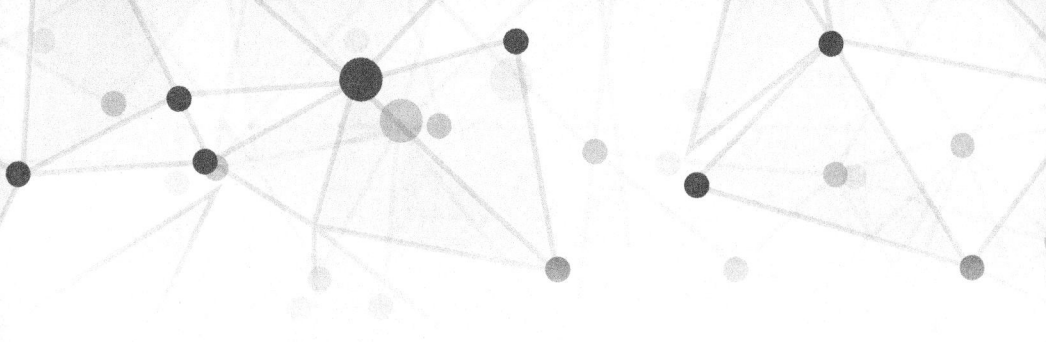

5

Fullerenes Past, Present and Future

"One of the most spiritual experiences any of us in the original team of five have ever experienced"
Richard Smalley - Fullerenes C60 Nobel Prize winner.

Fullerenes are considered a key component that makes Shungite stand out from every other mineral or crystal form, within its ability fullerenes can perform multiple contradictory functions in various settings ranging from general health and wellbeing, medicine, agriculture and industrial research. The western medical community has been particularly interested in studying the healing effects of fullerenes over the last five to ten years. A simple internet search for 'fullerenes' followed by a medical condition can often yield numerous studies highlighting the benefits of fullerenes that can be found naturally in Shungite.

Free full colour picture resources available at
www.shungiteexpectmiracles.me

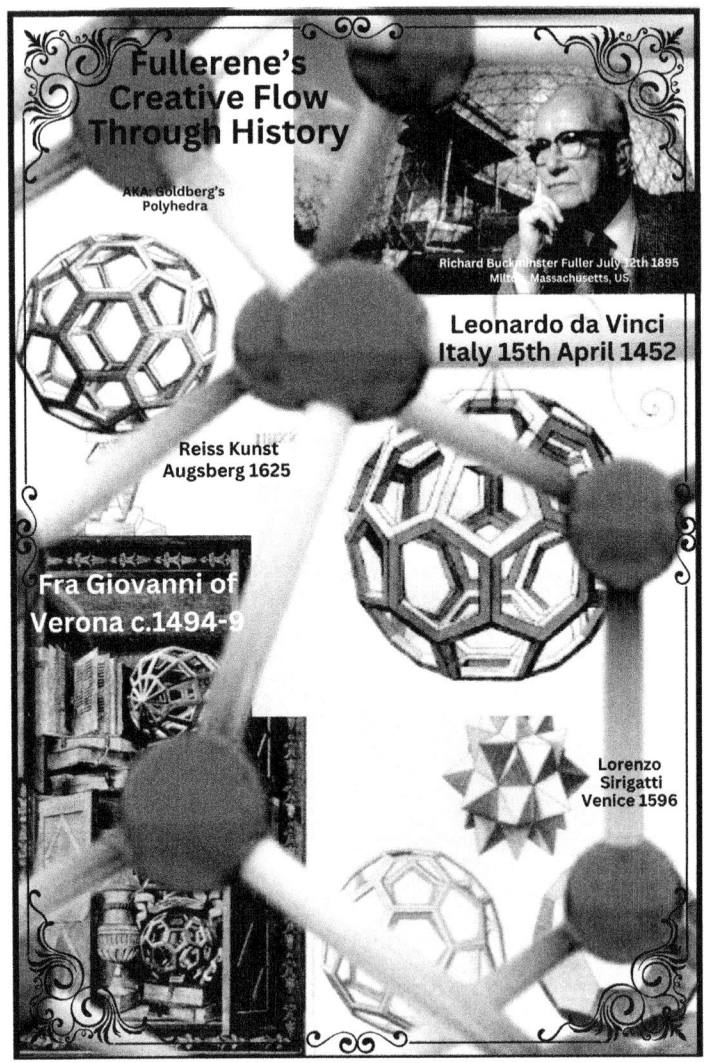

> "The C60 is a finite object linked to the infinite power
> of the quantum Field."
> Nancy L Hopkins

Fullerenes have been measured spinning between 20-30 billion times per second, making them the fastest molecule in spin-motion ever recorded. Importantly they spin to the right; opposite to entropy and decay. According to Nancy L Hopkins, "*proto-energy is pulsed into the C60 shape, spinning the molecule at 20 billion times a second. That spinning causes an energy field of extreme stability and force to exist*" this energy opens and then shuts the door to the quantum field. An independent inventor named Frank asserted that due to the speed of the Spin the fullerenes are able to access *every* frequency which is why it is cited to be able to deliver its unique mineral balancing action to each cell in the body.

Torsion field physics as explored extensively by Kozyrev and later found by Hoagland explains that the *faster the spin the greater the ability to access hyper-dimensions.* The energy and information existing in higher physical dimensions is accessible in our third dimension only through the physical 'rotations' of mass. Whilst it is difficult to conceive that there is a spinning molecule inside Shungite stones, essentially the nature of every atom in and and around us that we perceive as solid, is in fact a frequency of vibrating emptiness- the smaller and deeper they are examined. Things are simply solid because we *think* they are!

Each fullerene does an incredible job of cleaning up because it has a vacuum inside that pulls toxins in whilst the outside attracts free radicals. These football shaped molecules have been replicated up to 70 times inside themselves like an onion to capture radioactive particles. Fullerenes are 30 times more effective than activated charcoal in neutralising free radicals.

Interestingly, within the range of sizes they are found these tiny molecules are the exact size that fits into the nooks and crannies of DNA and RNA (Ribonucleic acid), which makes them perfect for rebuilding damaged DNA and RNA. Think of fullerenes as scaffolding for the rebuilding and regeneration of your cells to take place whilst they are accessing the energy from the quantum realm.

Fullerenes have been extensively studied and are comprised of fused rings and conjugated bonds with a hybridization of sp^2 and sp^3 bonds, with their average bond length of the single bond being 0.145 nm and the double bond that is 0.141 nm (Zhang et al. 1991); Fullerenes bear a truncated icosahedral symmetry because of which every carbon atom environment remains identical. Fullerene C60 has the smallest cage structure which makes it highly reactive. It is also highly stable as it follows the isolated pentagon rule which states that all the pentagons are surrounded by 5 hexagons. They are electron deficient, because of poor electron delocalization, which makes them a potent antioxidant and are becoming widely used in cancer therapy as stated by Prato in 1997 and also Echegoyen in 1998 hence, giving it the term 'free radical sponge'.

Fullerenes can undergo a lot of chemical reactions because they are electron acceptors, the conclusion being that the fullerenes are able to give and take, as the 'diseased' molecule is lacking electrons and Shungite gives them and can take away excess electrons, using the free radical cells to create more complex structures needed by the body whilst passing the spent cells attracted to the fullerenes through the urine. Due to its inertness, a lot of ionic species can be enclosed in its cage-like structure, with several distinct properties of being highly hydrophobicity, and with high cohesivity between fullerene molecules, photoactivity, and also high reactivity, they have an ability to accept and release electrons allowing varied chemical transformations and structural modifications for extensive biomedical use.

Research also shows that fullerenes can absorb electromagnetic energy which is great news for Shungite as it contains the same fullerenes; this adsorbing of artificial Wi-Fi frequencies will be protecting the body's nervous system. The question remains - where does the electromagnetic energy and toxins go when they are absorbed?

As science uncovers more mysteries about the fullerenes capabilities, Shungite also appears to break more rules and astound more people with its abilities too, as many more medical studies find that Shungite and fullerenes are able to rectify a wide range of problems. The way Shungite interacts with the human nervous system for one is a fascinating example. Whilst our nerves serve as the highway for electrical impulses that transmit pain, pleasure and movement sensations throughout the body, new research indicates that nerve impulses travel at a rate that surpasses the physical nerve highway's capability, similarly the way Shungite is also accessing an unseen source of energy, there must be additional networks being utilised by the bodies energy that has not been recognised by mainstream western science before.

Cassie worked with Nerve Professor Fiona Boissonade at Sheffield University on a funded collaboration to create a fully immersive walk-in interactive installation showcasing the vital role of nerves, their functions and repair cycles, exhibiting at the 'Festival of the Mind' International Science Expo. However, she later discovered that it's impossible for *all* electrical signals to follow the exact physical routes through the axons inside the myelin sheath because they simply travel too quickly, they must accessing some other invisible network, and this seems to be what Shungite is also doing, its accessing the quantum field bringing repairing frequencies on another paradigm network.

Another intriguing phenomenon linked to the mysterious topic of nerves is phantom limb syndrome, where people feel sensations in a limb after its amputation, where there are simply no nerves there that can fire electrical impulses to create *feelings*; Cassie has used Shungite pyramids made by Rich to activate healing on the injury site of the missing limbs on a number of people resulting in full physical sensations of healing in the absence of the limb, the Shungite is accessing this non physical network.

Shungite does infuse our aura with its energy, which spins at an incredible 20-30 billion times per second. This supercharged aura effectively transforms the negative left-hand spin of artificial Wi-Fi and mobile signals, resulting in a positive environment. However, the strength of your energy field is critical in maintaining this protection, and this is where silver activated Shungite plays a vital role in protecting deeper vital parts of our body and has a stronger effect on the outer aura making it a far superior compound for our needs.

Walt Silva is a scientist and experimenter who has worked for over 30 years seeing the connections and relationships between things that are mostly unseen by others. He states that "*the spiritual, the mental, and the physical affect each other; it is a non-stop reciprocal relationship.*" This also aligns with Oraphim's perspective that the relationship between the question, inquirer and answer are integral, we must keep an inquiring mind.

The National Institute of Health (NIH) has published additional studies that delve deeper into the topic of fullerene structures. According to one study that stated "We demonstrated the shape memory nanolens array that contains fullerenes not only to absorb electromagnetic energy but also to reinforce the Nano-structure. In particular, Young's modulus of the composite was enhanced by more than ten times by incorporating fullerenes into SMPs."

In 1979, Richard Buckminster Fuller conceived and developed this football shaped structure into buildings; these shapes were named after him and it these 'fullerenes' that were later discovered in Shungite in 1992, what still is a mystery is the fact that all Shungite stones work the way fullerenes work even if they actually posses any fullerenes or not, this leads to the understanding that Shungite stones are portal stones able to access the energy created by the fullerenes that are still in the quantum realm.

Cassie at Oraphim began her Shungite journey in 2002 by creating giant fullerenes, inspired by R Buckminister Fuller's geodesic architecture she made hers so that many others could meet, share and create wonderful experiences inside these geodomes at community events and festivals with many magical and mystical connections made; it's a wonderful coincidence that both Cassie and Richard Buckminsterfuller share the 12th of July as their birthdays.

Cassie together with Rich have developed their fullerenes to have evolved from over 60 broom handles to architecturally beautiful bamboo structures that span eight metres and are held together with only 11 bolts, requiring only 20 poles. These structures can be erected and dismantled quickly by people of all ages! People who spend time in Cassie's and Rich's fullerenes-inspired marques experience something special. Their wishes can come true, their moods lift, they are creative and joyful, and even the coffee served in these spaces has been described as *'the best coffee at the event'.* Unlike other structures that cannot withstand storms nearly as well, this fullerenes-inspired marque is firmly rooted into the earth and remains unscathed in the toughest conditions, what she has later come to realise is that just by water being inside the fullerene geodome it was being altered by the fullerenes form to taste better, and that people are mostly water which is why they also are energetically transformed too.

Many artists have been fascinated by geometric and platonic shapes, and the 'fullerene' was actually depicted many hundreds of years ago, before its modern iteration as a 'fullerene' its technical name is a truncated icosahedron later named Goldberg's Polyhedra.

The earliest illustrations of polyhedra depicted in the form of 'solid edges' were sketched by Leonardo Da Vinci. The solidity of the edges lets one easily see which edges belong to the front and which to the back, unlike simple line drawings where the front and back surfaces may be visually confused. Yet the hollow faces allow one to see through to the structure of the rear surface. This is a brilliant new form of geometric illustration, one worthy of Leonardo's genius for insightful graphic display of information. However, it is not clear whether Leonardo invented this new form or whether he was simply drawing from 'life' a series of wooden models with solid edges which Pacioli designed. If Pacioli designed these models, then he deserves the credit for this new 'solid edge' idea, but it is asserted that it is likely that Leonardo designed them himself.

An Exploration of the Historical and Modern Significance of Fullerenes and Shungite

- F Giovanni's stunning woodcuts, composed between the years 1494-99 are installed in a Verona church which were inspired from the drawings above by Da Vinci.

- David Wade's collection of Renaissance polyhedral and artistic visions, featured in 'Fantastic Geometry', featuring beautifully drawn images by Reiss Kunst (Augsburg 1625).

- In 1985 Robert F Curl, Harold W Kroto and Richard E Smalley along with James R Heath and Sean O'Brien created the world's first laboratory-made synthetic C_{60} and C_{70} fullerenes using a laser to vaporise coal dust and this released carbon atoms mixed with helium gas.

- For some the excitement comes when they discover the news that the fullerene C_{60}s can affect the 'telomeres' in the body by drastically reducing oxidative stress leading to longevity.

- In 1992 Semyon Tsipursky and Peter Buseck discovered the existence of both C60 and C70 in Shungite rocks using an electron microscope.

- In 1998 C60 fullerenes were found to inhibit the replication of the HIV virus in rats; whilst in 2007 they were shown to kill cancer cells.

- In 2012 rats given synthesised C60 suspended in olive oil lived 90% longer, demonstrating the potential benefits of fullerenes for human health.

- Snake venom is able to target the weakest organ in our system which in a compromised body will cause rapid ill health and even death, this is why it is used in covert assassination; Snake venom has also been reported to cause mood alterations, lethargy, blurring of vision and alterations in the nervous system but fullerenes were studied and proven to be an effective antivenom when used as a preventative and also when used as a restorative to detoxify from the poison in a study with crickets.

Although artificial fullerenes (C60) are available on the market their high production cost makes them extremely expensive and in the opinion of Nancy L Hopkins and Regina Martino they pale in comparison to the natural versions found in Shungite.

What is interesting to note are the immense temperatures it takes to create the fullerenes in the first place, as this likely also dispels the theory that Shungite was formed naturally from decomposing biological matter. In Johnathan Hare's YouTube mini-lecture describing the creation of synthesised fullerenes the bell jar is filled with helium which is then sparked with 100 or 200 amps at 50 volts to create an arc producing temperatures of 2000 - 3000 degrees creating the soot from the carbon rods to obtain fullerenes; so it is simply easier to pick up some Shungite stones instead when your wanting to work with fullerenes.

In 1997 Mr Djuro Koruga patented fullerene onions where his layered fullerenes trap radiation to create a radiation absorbing storage molecule. It comprises a Buckminsterfullerene C60 molecule and a radioactive material encapsulated within the molecule. The C60 molecule has an electronically closed shell and rotates at a minimum speed of 3×10^{10} s^{-1} to trap the harmful radiation; this patent is the proof that the fullerenes do have a record breaking spin speed as well as the start of the journey to cleaning up our toxic world of radioactive materials.

The Role of Shungite Fullerenes in Cancer Recovery

Oraphim have seen several cases of cancer recovery since working with Shungite, as it has played an important role in their recovery process.

The benefits have included a significant increase in the white blood cell count and the prevention of their blood from becoming abnormally 'deranged' just from wearing a silver activated Shungite pendant. Whilst meeting others who have personally told of their miraculous use of Shungite simply by placing it on the tumours and within a couple of weeks the cancerous mass simply vanished.

In another remarkable case a cancer surgery that was expected to take four hours to remove extensive lymphatic tissue only took 1 hr 30 minutes in total, because the damaged tissues were substantially less than had previously been planned for removal. The patient recovered smoothly and miraculously with substantially fewer lymph nodes removed than anticipated. As a result she is currently in full recovery.

Fullerenes are now being found to target and isolate cancer cells with the potential to not be causing harmful side effects, with scientists talking about replacing chemotherapy treatments which cause many ill side effects as they also exhibit dose-limiting toxicity and non-specific toxicity to healthy cells, with alopecia, anorexia, peripheral neuropathy, and diarrhoea being the distinctive short term side effects and leave lasting damage to the recovering patient; with one study published by the NIH stating that 'C70[>M(C3N6 +C3)2] being more effective at cancer cell killing than C60[>M(C3N6 +C3)2]'; C70's are more prevalently found in Elite Shungite stones and this also corresponds with the anecdotal testimonials of people placing the elite stones near the tumours and them disappearing in very short amount of time; this is great news for a greater future filled with Shungite and healthy people.

An additional study conducted by Nie et al. came up with $C60(OH)22$ nano-particles, which were found to be highly efficacious in the treatment of cancer. What was found was that fullerenes in the $C60(OH)22$ nano-particles state had the potential to block and also attenuate the damaged 4T1 cells and stem cell interactions thereby significantly suppressing tumour growth and such metastasis. It was known that proliferation and metastasis of tumours are promoted by the interactions between neoplastic cells and mesenchymal stem cells derived from the bone marrow. Also, it was found that 4T1 cancer cells of the breast could induce malignant differentiation of the stem cells which in turn influenced 4T1 cell growth and metastasis which is the development of secondary malignant growths at a distance from a primary site of cancer, and this is what is stated as being halted by the special C60 fullerenes in their experiments.

With further studies by Liu and colleagues who devised a metal-fullerenol-based nano-particle (Gd@C82(OH)22), which displayed an intrinsic inhibitory activity against triple-negative breast tumours while not causing any toxicity to normal epithelial cells of the mammary gland. With astounding results being recording from studies performed within the biological subject where in just 2 weeks using the fullerene nano-composite (Gd@C82(OH)22) which is a water-soluble fullerenes more than a 40% decrease in the tumour density was displayed, its fascinating to report that fullerenes show distinctive tumour growth inhibition and promotes immune system up-regulation and these Polyhydroxy fullerenes molecules have a size of 1.3 nm which can be easily excreted in urine; literally the tumours are dispersing and disappearing at a rapid rate in a natural and harmless way.

Free full colour picture resources available at
www.shungiteexpectmiracles.me

Dr. Nina Kolesnikova & team produced remarkable results with patients at the sanatorium near Moscow

Specialising in cardiology, diabetes, hypertension, infectious diseases, the patients **needed much less medication overall** and an excerpt from the study showed that patients **blood levels returned to normal within two weeks** following their cancer radiation treatment when drinking shungite water for the control group this took an average of 3-4 months to return to normal.

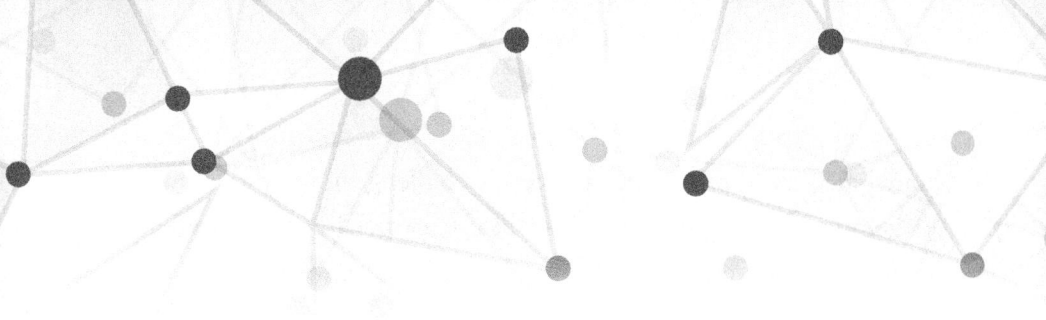

6

Shungite Powder and Purifying Stones for Everyday Health

Shungite powder possesses incredible healing properties that can be beneficial for anyone looking to detoxify their body. How much is needed? Take guidance from the stones themselves. When held in the hands the black stones release a little natural dust, this can be seen as a beautiful indication for just how powerful a little of the powder is in small doses.

Published in Regina Martino's Book 'Shungite-Protection, Healing and Detoxification' there are detailed many medical examinations of patients experiences with Shungite including the healing of the Digestive tract with just 100 ml of Shungite water, Steam inhalations curing COPD, Skin and arthritic conditions getting rapid relief and the vital organs being vitally supported through radiation treatments just to name a few.

However, bridging the gap between laboratory and medical studies and practical application has been a challenge for many; whilst a large number of western studies will use artificially synthesised C60 Fullerenes; Shungite can be used as a natural and highly effective alternative which is also much more cost effective. That's where Oraphim comes in as they have developed various ways to utilise Shungite and make it accessible to people in their day-to-day lives. As a result many people have been sharing their life changing testimonials.

Even in small doses Shungite powder which is naturally occurring on the stones is highly efficient at detoxifying and enhancing mineral functions. A simple bowl of steaming Shungite water with a towel over your head can be a highly effective way to conduct a Shungite steam inhalation to aid the fullerenes to get into the respiratory system, these have been found to be effective in treating the common cold, strep infections and conditions like COPD which is caused by mould spores (which is a common factor in many homes) even alleviating the use of inhalers. Additionally, fullerenes have 500 times more potent antioxidants than Vitamin C and can accumulate in the body unlike Vitamin C which is discarded if not used within 24 hours.

Unlike artificially manufactured C60 molecules Shungite is water soluble and possesses a life force. Some people find mixing the powder with raw natural honey is an easy, hassle-free way to aid ingestion; with the hexagonal structure of the Shungite fullerenes complementing the bee's honeycomb's hexagonal shapes making it a perfect combination.

Adding a pinch to your favourite health shakes or drinks is a fine addition. There was once an on-line Shungite recipe book which even had black Shungite bread in it. Putting some powder into a jar lid and placing it at the entrance to the bees hive has many advantages for both the bees and us, the bee colonies experience far less disease and infestations from other bugs, colony collapse syndrome is also eradicated and the pollination of the whole surrounding environment undergoes rapid expansion according to the meticulous observations and recordings of the difference the Shungite powder made to Derrick Condit's bee colonies.

Hot Honey Cold/Flu Remedy (Roberta's Recipe)

Ingredients

1 pot Raw Honey

3 x Garlic

2 inch Ginger or 2 tsp powder

2 inch Turmeric or 2 tsp powder

1 inch chilli chopped or powder 1 tsp

Black Pepper, 2 grinds to activate Turmeric.

1 tsp Black shungite powder

Wash, chop and steep all ingredients in honey in a large sterile jar. Keep in the dark for one week or longer. Sieve and pot up when ready.

For Colds and Flu

Take one tsp of honey in hot water or use it in tea to stimulate your immune system and clear out congestion. When you go to bed, place slices of raw potatoes in your socks, this will draw out toxins and by morning you should feel well.

To Decongest Lungs

As well as using steam inhalation to breath in beneficial Shungite water vapour by using a bowl of hot water with a towel over your head, you may like to make a great tasting tea with Lungwort, Mullian and Thyme Leaves, it can also be added to soups and stews and will help to decongest Lungs. Add 1 tiny pinch black shungite when consuming.

Flour free fruit and nut pudding or energy bars.

1 lb organic mixed fruit

1 lb dates

4 oz Goji Berries

1lb organic mixed nuts

1 inch Ginger or 1 tsp powder

I inch cinnamon stick, grind up

1 tsp mixed spice

1/2 organic lemon

1 tsp Black shungite powder.

Put all dried fruits (except goji berries) into water to soak overnight. Soak goji berries separately.

Drain and rinse. Put all ingredients except goji berries into the blender. Blend, then stir in goji berries, lemon juice and black shungite. You may like to add 1 tot brandy to the mix, for Xmas pudding taste. Spread mixture in a pan lined with greaseproof paper and bake on low at 100 degrees for 8 hours to dehydrate for energy bars or serve as a pudding with homemade ice cream or chia seed pudding.

Shungite has been noted to be able to reverse the 'intoxication' of alcohol's effects too, so add some stones to your drinks or a Oraphim Toggle to the bottles it even makes a cheap wine taste expensive.

Shungite powder has been found to be effective in detoxing the body of symptoms related to snake venom poisoning which is generally not a significant concern in the developed world but recent research studies have shown that the symptoms of 'C_vid19' match exactly those of snake venom poisoning. Shungite powder can help detoxify the body and promote hair growth; making it an effective remedy for those experiencing hair loss from what is being cited as the symptoms of 'C_vid'.

Adding a pinch of Shungite powder to products around the home such as shampoo, conditioner, liquid soap and detergents can help neutralise chemicals and enhance their cleaning abilities; also creating a pleasant aroma when none was present before.

Different shungite growing information: Studies have shown that watering seeds with shungite water can accelerate their germination, growth and development. Adding 10 grams of shungite to 1 m 2 of soil can provide plants with many mineral nutrition elements. In the soil for indoor plants, you can add 10 g of shungite powder per 1 kg of substrate. Crushed stone is used as drainage and at the same time for feeding indoor and garden plants. The use of shungite is economically very profitable and does not require large capital expenditures.

Its remarkable healing properties can also be used to quickly heal mouth and gum ulcers, but continued use can cause tooth stains, however the staining can be removed by using a teeth whitening stain remover.

Utilising Shungite powder to create heat-conducting, current-conducting Shungite paint that consumes very little energy is easy to do. In addition, this mineral is eco-friendly, does not emit harmful substances, and is not flammable, its use reduces the cost of heating as was confirmed by Becky when she used the Silver activated Shungite powder for her son's bedroom, which is now a much warmer room than it was before, helping to make substantial savings on their heating bills with only 50 gms of powder used. With reports it has been used to replace traditional Underfloor heating that creates electromagnetic radiation, simply by using environmental Shungite which is the cheapest building grade of Shungite available. Another option is to coat ceramic tiles, or carpet floor tiles, with the back side painted with Shungite infused paint. Any surface lined with such conductive tiles acts like a well-insulated electric stove and works in the same principle as expensive thermo ceramic vacuum additives available on the decorating market, because Shungites' fullerenes also have a vacuum. One of the unique properties of Shungite used in construction is that this rock is not magnetic, but is electrically conductive.

Industry has already mastered Shungite materials that absorb electromagnetic radiation from high and low temperatures and now is a great time to infuse your own living environments with it too. Shungite has been found to be used in the construction of premises that require the protection of confidential information. Shungite has even been used to protect safes with state and Bank secrets, as it localises information leaks, serving as a reliable screen for any new radar devices and intelligence tools which may be useful to note when wanting to protect your own home from invasive 5G. In ordinary rooms it is possible to obtain a shielding effect by adding the silver activated Shungite powder to plaster and paint or using it to make special Shungite tiles or plates as outlined above. These properties of Shungite are especially valuable for corporations whose offices have a lot of computers. It has been stated that the Shungite walls in such an office are able to completely absorb electromagnetic radiation. For example, some Japanese companies are interested in building such environmentally friendly premises that simultaneously harmonise the internal state of a person, and even Oraphim used the silver activated Shungite powder to give an enhancing, protective and renovating layer to their own work space in Balby.

Shungite powder can also be used in art projects such as printing, painting or as was used in ancient times by making it into ink; it's only limitation is our imagination, you can get inspiration by checking out Oraphim's Shungite infused Fabric paints for your own DIY protection projects too.

There is conclusive evidence that man-made electromagnetic frequencies must be adjusted to be biocompatible and to counteract the imbalances that cause illness in the human body. For example, our overexposure to Wi-Fi is causing acute EMF sensitivity which is presenting as Chronic Fatigue Syndrome (CFS), Myalgic Encephalitis (ME) and Multiple Sclerosis (MS). This is due to the fact that the harmful frequencies have a left hand spin known as 'entropy', which breaks down the myelin sheath that covers our nervous system and causes it to leak proteins into other systems in the body.

Posted on an obscure chat board Cassie was reading that antihistamines were helpful in treating ME and MS and she had often wondered why Shungite was such a powerful antihistamine. Oraphim subsequently found that Shungite, which contains fullerenes, can rapidly repair the nerves' myelin sheath because of this natural and powerful antihistamine action. The fullerenes in Shungite absorb the microwave irradiation, which is confirmed by Dancook University in Korea; thus protecting the nerves from further damage so that the body can repair and heal.

Shungite has an almost immediate effect with people noticing rejuvenation even on the first day of wearing a Shungite pendant of any grade Shungite. The level of rapid recovery and healing from Multiple Sclerosis is also remarkable and almost miraculous; they are regaining their quality of life, where they can walk and garden again after being severely limited or confined to a wheelchair.

Ultimately we want better connectivity when it comes to mobile technology without the damaging effects. In conventional circumstances this would require the frequency to be entirely blocked to protect the human body from the 'waves' but when this is not possible, we need to alter the 'wave' in a way that corrects its effects from negative to positive and to mop up any waves affecting the myelin sheath. Changing the quality of information sent through the airwaves allows technology to continue to work well and reported by many to actually work much better with silver activated Shungite, and this traditionally would break the 'laws of physics'.

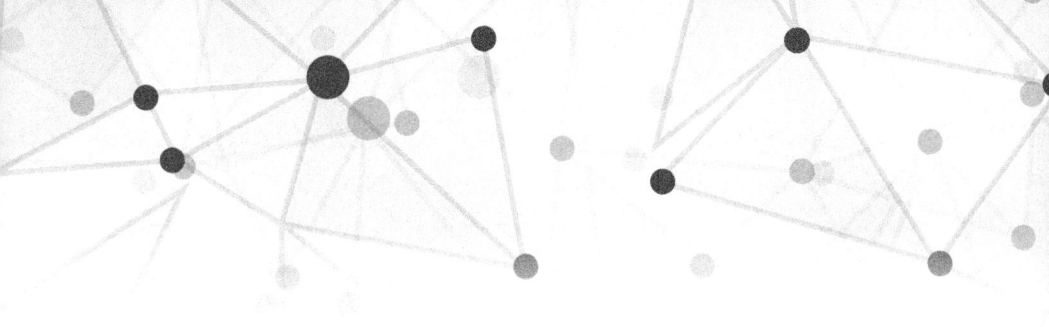

7

The Art of Dowsing: Shungite Effects the Energy Body

For those unfamiliar with dowsing it's a technique that enables access to information from the subconscious mind that would otherwise be difficult to obtain. Our subconscious is intricately connected through our higher self to the Universal Knowledge, Universal Consciousness or The Field as described extensively by Rupert Sheldrake and Lynne McTaggart. To access this field we use what's called the Ideomotor Response, which usually manifests as tiny movements in our hands. Dowsing tools such as pendulums, L rods and Y rods amplify this response making it visible and tangible.

You don't need to spend a lot of money on dowsing tools as they can be easily crafted at home using everyday materials, for L-rods repurpose metal coat hangers. To create a pendulum take some child's putty like Play Dough or blue tack, roll it into a ball and insert a string or cord. Allow it to harden overnight; alternatively a pendant or plumb bob used for wallpapering can also work. There's really no need to use special materials like crystals or copper for rods, but some dowsers may have a preference for them and others who have used Shungite pendulums have rated them higher than other crystal versions they have used before.

Chris Quartermaine's fascination with Shungite began when he attended a British Society of Dowsers conference where a lecture on the subject was given; he shares his experiences "we were given several Shungite samples to dowse over and I was thoroughly impressed. This led me to purchase a small Shungite pyramid for myself. Upon returning home I started conducting experiments of my own. One such exercise I typically teach beginner dowsers is to use rods to measure the aura of their partner. The crucial thing to remember about dowsing is that it only works when you create a clear intention in your mind whilst holding the tools. The dowser stands a few metres away from the partner and slowly moves towards them, focusing on the intention that the rods will cross when reaching their outer aura. I have found that this approach tends to work for most people."

This exercise is easily replicated as Chris explains further "I decided to try this exercise with the Shungite and mark the outer aura. Then, I handed them an unprotected mobile phone and asked them to hold it against their heart whilst switched on, and measured their aura again. The results were staggering, with a significant reduction in the outer aura being observed. However, when I gave them a piece of Shungite to hold alongside the phone and measured the aura again, it usually reverted to its original size, or even increased in size on occasion. Subsequent tests have yielded similar outcomes, demonstrating the amazing properties of Shungite."

Chris concludes that "our experiment yielded some interesting results, demonstrating how different types of Shungite and their sizes can impact their effectiveness. We found that Elite Shungite consistently outperformed other types to affect the aura field in a beneficial way, and that we found size truly matters. Additionally our test of Oraphim's mobile phone stickers with the silver activated Shungite showed that they too were more effective than plain Shungite. You can even try this experiment yourself without a mobile phone. Simply keep Shungite on your person and observe the expansion of your aura. Give it a go!"

Chris had an interesting experience to share "When I first purchased my Shungite pyramid, I proudly displayed it on my router in my office. However, a psychic friend of mine soon detected a negative presence in the room that needed to be eradicated; (the pyramid was not silver infused or Elite.) After using dowsing I was shocked to discover that my Shungite pyramid was the source of the negativity; it seems to have attracted or quarantined some negative frequencies. Further research revealed that intermediate black Shungite, which was used to make the pyramid, is more susceptible to becoming 'dirty' compared to Elite Shungite. To cleanse it I am now able to use various methods such as leaving it under a tap or near an amethyst crystal. However, my preferred method was to use intention to heal it whilst holding it in my hands. It's important to note that Elite Shungite contains 98% carbon, which makes it less likely to become 'dirty' and cause negativity in the environment and Oraphim do add this same Elite powder into their creations."

As our modern lives are so consumed by technology it's understandable that more people are suffering from EMF exposure, and new health alerts are being issued to raise awareness of the harmful side effects. Oraphim has developed teaching and engagement activities for young people to help them integrate the latest knowledge on the subject so that they can make more informed choices when it comes to recreational activities that use screens.

During their educational sessions Cassie and Rich lead activities to empower better emotional insights and motivational choices, recently working with the 'Universal Kidz' project in Stockport (UK) Cassie planned an activity around emotional motivation and why we want the things we want; and why we want to experience certain activities and experiences along side EMF meter readings and recording of electrical equipment in the building and dowsing each other.

The students at Universal Kidz have prepared the following report from their dowsing experiments:

Item to be dowsed	Amelia	Adelia
Just them alone	19m	40m
With a mobile phone	6m	6.5m
Phone and Bosnian Orgonite	12M	100+m
Phone With Anti Radiation Image	14m	100+
Phone Shungite Stickers	15m	-
Phone Shungite polish	15m	-
Phone Elite Shungite	17m	-
With just Bosnian Organite	17M	-

Findings:

With this very quick dowsing experiment, which is good for engaging most people in experiencing changes in energy field systems, we had Adelia whose energy field expanded tremendously with the addition of the EMF correcting materials which meant she got bored very quickly waiting around for the measuring to take place, so this resulted in only a few results getting measured and recorded. Emelia (AKA-Epic Raspberry) being three years older had a smaller field sadly already but much more patience.

The other dowsing team made up of James, Jonas and Niah found that they were picking up on buried water pipes which was affecting the dowsing so sadly could not take any measurements, which was likely their own resonant body water in coherence with the water in the pipes.

The simple key to everything is that we are motivated by emotional cues. The group explored their wants and desires on a Christmas present wish list and imagined plans for growing into adulthood. They recognised that everything is generally both emotional and physical, as most things generate an emotional response and often fulfil a physical action or requirement at the same time. Emotional intelligence is key to being in control of our desires. The younger members of the group focused on creating emotionally rich drawings of characters who were both stuck in doors surrounded by technology screens. They decided that this was more lonely and unhappy when compared to the mirror of this being happy playing out in the parks with friends and animals.

Conclusions to consider:

What we can see is that both Chris Quartermaine and the Universal Kidz dowsing results highlighted that the Elite Shungite responded better for aura expansion as they both found the Elite does have a very strong effect on the energy field of the body, as well as the Shungite silver activated stickers that are also alleviating the harm and boosting the field as the mobile phone is held, along with the anti radiation image and Bosnia Orgonite.

What we do note however is that there are limitations to this testing method as we have explored other testing methodologies such as the autonomic response testing which highlights more deeply the effect of the negative frequencies on the internal organs and it is this that is not expressed through the dowsing method. Also Nancy L

Hopkins and Walt Silva's experiments showed silver infused Shungite is capable of extraordinary transformations with a single reset to the devices, you can always be sure that Shungite is ready to show you what it can do when you play and interact with it.

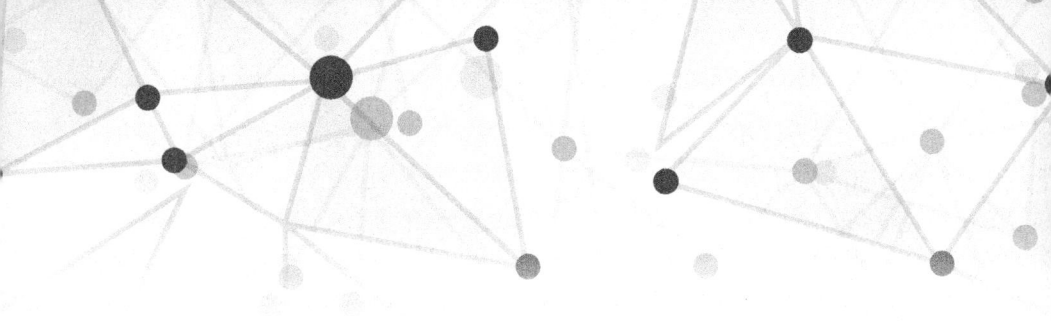

8

Superior Silver Activated Shungite

"Integrity is the essence of everything successful."
R Buckminster Fuller

Nancy L Hopkins was joined by Walt Silva in the development of silver treated Shungite powder which they named S4 and this new compound resulted in a number of remarkable enhancements. Nancy L Hopkins was a Wi-Fi Warfare Officer in the US Military; she has since published astonishing thermographic photos that clearly showed the negative effects of mobile phone calls to the head and the reduction in radiation damage when a silver activated Shungite sticker was applied. This unique phenomenon was due to a special combination that they developed, this new compound vastly reduces necrosis in the head of the person making the call. Oraphim learned about this compound and they reproduced it in the UK; they have been able to help in proving that it changed the quality and direction of the electromagnetic information received by the body in several ways.

Registered Nurse Caron Barr conducted a live blood analysis study and discovered that a cluster of six stem cells were seen to be present during the examination; she explained that stem cells are never found in adults - yet there they were. The blood cells were seen to stack up when the mobile cell phone was used with Nancy's S4 Sticker applied to the phone as is usual for Wi-Fi to affect the blood in this way, but remarkably a cleaning process began straight away, as rapidly white blood cells came along to detoxify the damaged cells and they were released from the stacking in super quick time.

Kenneth Wheeler discussed at length on his in depth and fascinating YouTube channel 'Theoria Apophasis;' that essentially what is commonly referred to as EMF waves is only an unseen medium which is perturbed by energy frequencies. Although the effect is described as 'waves,' these frequencies are simply creating movement in this unseen medium called the 'aether.' The addition of silver has a reversing as well as an enhancing effect on the aether which results in less damage to the body and better signals from both artificial and biological devices.

In 2019, a paper was published by a group from Kyiv's National University of Food Technology collaborating with the Bakul Institute of Super hard Materials at the National Academy of Sciences of Ukraine, concluding that a process of steam activation and nano silver infusion increased Shungite's abilities to purify water. This process raised its absorption properties and increased the efficiency of water treatment during beverage production resulting in the stabilisation of the redox potential of the prepared water. Excessive amounts of redox active chemicals are damaging to the body and this reactive oxygen can overthrow redox balance which can lead to cellular disease conditions or death which is why it's so important that silver enhanced Shungite affects this in an even more positive way.

Adding this silver enhanced Shungite powder to paint for EMF harmonising of homes, workspaces and healing sanctuaries is highly beneficial, creating the maximum frequency transformation to your environments. Comments have come back from restaurants and family homes having enjoyed a remarkably beautiful calm and happy time especially over the winter festive periods! Oraphim suggests mixing around 50 gm of silver activated powder with a little paint or PVA glue into a paste, then adding it to your 2.5L pot of paint; bear in mind that this will slightly darken your colour when selecting colour shades and using it as the base coat with your final coat to give a great finish is often preferable.

Shungite has shown that it does not have to be physically in contact with the water to transform it as feedback from people putting Oraphim stickers on water pipes was published in 'Shungite Reality - A Study of Energy,' by N L Hopkins. A similar testimonial from a customer led Cassie to put into production a more durable banded toggle, which simply attaches with the band around taps and water bottles, your hair, wrist, animal water bottles or anywhere else you can think of. This toggle is made with the silver activated Shungite powder, and in the water analysis tests, it was the best-performing chlorine nullifier.

Here's the happy story of Merlin an old adoptee cat who was deathly sick and thin to the bones when his owner first adopted him, the owner gave him a normal Shungite stone piece on its collar for its first six months with her which helped him with multiple problems, some disappearing completely and keeping the inflammation level in check. Merlin had been wearing his new Oraphim pretty collar for a week, and she reported that all the positive effects witnessed with the non-silver activated Shungite had more than doubled, most notably in terms of energy levels. The owner highly recommends silver activated Shungite to anyone who wishes to keep their pets from getting sick or help them cure from illness; this is the difference between the two as shown by Merlin's rapid recovery and even more amazing advances since his Oraphim collar arrived, think how remarkable the results could be for you and your family.

Conclusion: *ALL* Shungite stones are uniquely powerful being unlike any other stones on the planet. Black Shungite is phenomenal, it goes beyond our normal references of effectiveness, providing tangible results rapidly- that is why it's amazing, but the Silver activated Shungite powder is the most effective compound to date for its overall enhanced abilities.

It is with great appreciation to Nancy L Hopkins and her team for their advances and work in this field of Shungite, information and Wi-Fi warfare.

Many people witness an instant effect when applying an Oraphim sticker to electrical devices such as modems and routers, this can cause them to 'reset' which is annoying for kids playing on games when this frequency is flipped to be better the moment the sticker is applied! And laptops can experience a significant increase in internet connectivity when just one Oraphim Shungite sticker is applied to the router. Whilst additional Shungite stickers may be necessary for certain device models of mobile handsets; if it's still getting hot add another sticker and see the difference; 'smart' meters require a full nine stickers in a geometric triangular pattern as asserted by Nancy L Hopkins, the silver-activated Shungite's ability to enhance and transform one's own 'field' using only very small amounts of such a valuable resource makes it an effective quantum solution for EMF protection without the worry of depleting the Earth's resources as it only takes a pinch per appliance.

One lady testified that when her iPhone accidentally went through a wash cycle it came out working perfectly *both* times. She claims that the Shungite sticker saved it, Oraphim doesn't suggest you try this at home, but how fascinating!

5 out of 5 stars

LISTING REVIEW BY JULS

"Bought the stickers and used them on electronic devices and in shoes. It works!! Am amazed my feet don't feel 'tired' after many hours of walking and back ache I had was not there anymore. Place 2 stickers on the Wi-Fi router and on our iPhones, wish had more stickers. Will definitely come back to get more in the near future. Super happy! So glad I found Oraphim! Thank you Cassie, Richard and team. God bless" Juls 21 May, 2022 5 out of 5 stars   MICHELLE VAN WYK

"Speedy delivery. I am gobsmacked. My laptop had not got hot today and neither had the charger. I can't quite believe it. I also placed one of these stickers on the kitchen tap. My children commented on the clean and lovely tasting water. This is an exceptional product. X"

4 out of 5 stars   STOMMENUIL

"I have quite a lot of these. I have them on my phone, kindle, and laptop and Wi-Fi router. They do work but you need a lot. I have 3 on my phone. Yes it doesn't get as hot as it used to but it still does get warm as do the kindle and the laptop. Having heard a comment in a video that Cassie made I have three on the back of my radiators, two downstairs and one up. These will influence the water in the radiator system. I do feel that there is a calmness in the house since they have been applied." Stommenuil 19 Mar, 2022

"Can't believe it, but our internet speeds are much faster, and I can now answer my phone at my desk. I could not do that before my Shungite sticker!" Dr H. Brew

"Thank you got them on time and I love it my mobile no longer heats up although I had to use 2 stickers on my Huawei Pro20 will purchase more"

"Great product! I used my pendulum to test the stickers and it does make them spin. There is good energy there. I plan to purchase more."

"I appreciate my stickers and the special gift for my shoes. I had to put 3 stickers on my Galaxy 8 plus in order for me to no longer feel pain in my hands. I can use my phone pain free."

"These are great. I can notice a difference in my office environment, and great value for money too."

"Arrived super-fast. On my phone already and doesn't seem to be getting so hot. A great price too. Thank you"

"Thank you so much! My phone is no longer overheating, and I mentally feel more protected!"

SILVER ACTIVATED SHUNGITE STICKERS
Made by Oraphim

Reverses harmful frequencies instantly *and* provides better connectivity

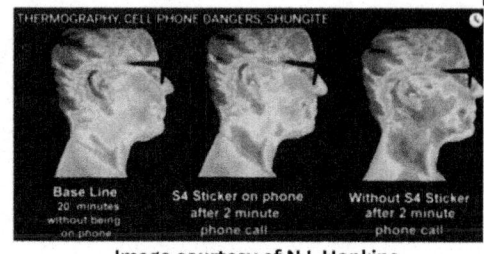

Full red head and neck

Image courtesy of N L Hopkins

"These are great I can notice a difference in my office environment, and great value for money too."

"Arrived super fast. On my phone already & doesn't seem to be getting so hot A great price too Thank you"

"Thank you so much! My phone is no longer overheating, and I mentally feel more protected! ♥"

<u>Michelle van Wyk</u> 04 Feb, 2021 5 out of 5 stars *"Speedy delivery. I am gobsmacked. My laptop had not got hot today and neither had the charger. I can't quite believe it. I also placed one of these stickers on the kitchen tap. My children commented on the clean and lovely tasting water. This is an exceptional product."*

Negative EMF Radiation Reduction

- **Simply Harmonize Your Phone**

- **Full 'SMART' Frequency Protection Today**

- **No Need to Replace, Cleanse or charge Silver Infused Shungite**

- *Wifi waves are spun back in line with Nature by Quantum Energy C60*

- **Ground your Bodies Energy Field back to nature Quantum lay-line grid connection**

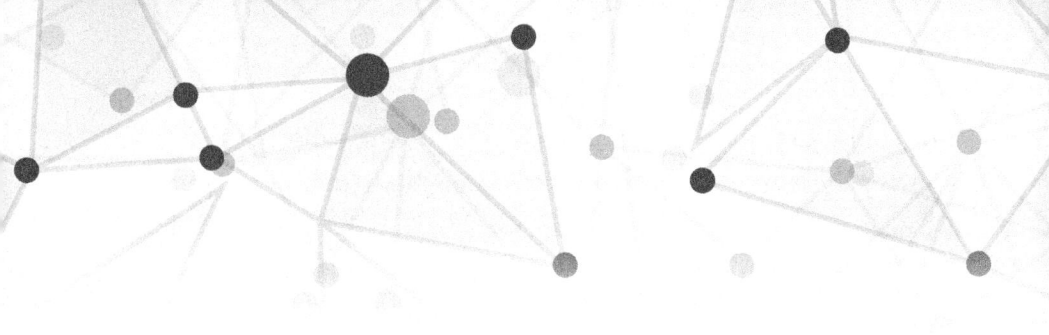

9

Breaking the Laws of Physics: The Modern Mystery

"It will likely surprise no one, to note the constantly growing interest in this domain. From substantial scientific papers up to the firmly based industrial production, the nanocarbon / epoxy composites will probably continue to surprise us for years to come."

Agnieszka D browska

Victor Georgievich Veselago a Russian physicist, published in 1967 theoretical analysis of materials with conductivity (negative permittivity.) and the ability to block energy simultaneously, damping of charge (permeability µ.v); he was literally referring to 'breaking the laws of physics' at the time of his writing and this is what is occurring with the magical mixture of silver and Shungite.

Shungite is a material that seems to contradict itself in many ways serving as an example of how laws can be broken. It possesses multiple opposite properties which does cause a lot of conflicting information in regards to its abilities; one example we will look at later on is its ability to nullify chemicals in water without removing them but also energises the water, because it is being both highly energetic and a neutralising substance, a reductant (electron-rich) with its ability to donate electrons to needy free radicals to neutralise them, whilst also being and an oxidant (electron hungry), it is found to be both hydrophilic (attracts water) and hydrophobic (repels water). It is also chemically potent and chemically inert, aliphatic (open chained) and aromatic (closed-chained), paramagnetic (attracted to magnetic fields like our body's) and diamagnetic (repulsed by magnetic fields) which is why our energy field expands, electrically conductive which can be seen when using a flat piece on your mobile phone screen and a dialectic which is not conductive but insulating and repelling which is why it is used to line the blast furnaces. It is a mineraloid with earthly origins, biogenic and also strangely not of earthly origins - abiogenic.

When people first encounter the claims that Shungite has they can understandably be very scathing and dismissive of its abilities to perform such opposing tasks, it defies logic. The contradictory behaviours required of a compound and subsequent product that claims to harmonise devices emitting negative energy *and* enhance man-made electromagnetic signals is contradictory and baffling to some, and not everyone is open to accepting that commonly taught and accepted laws of physics are changing at a rapid rate and they are simply unaware of these new developments in advancing physics.

Shungite's unique properties have proven great potential in various studies of electromagnetic and electronic application; by combining Shungite with silver in the way that Oraphim does, these compounds are called metamaterials also known as ENM's which are proven to create electromagnetic attenuation, shielding and repair as well as wave absorption.

In modern times we rely heavily on internet connectivity, but this comes at an unquantifiable cost to our health and all living things around us. Shungite that is processed and activated with silver and heat offers a solution that allows Wi-Fi signals to keep our technology connected without further interruption and with much less negative effects on our health. With many even experiencing enhanced effects such as faster internet and better connection which Oraphim's' silver activated Shungite stickers surprisingly provide.

Oraphim discovered that this innovative combination of different materials technically known as a 'metamaterial' does indeed produce a powerful effect. This compound is more than the sum of its parts as each element plays a unique role in the overall functionality of the products they produce.

> *"Similarly like Shungite you are also more than the sum of your cells".*
> States Cassie.

Starting with **silver**, a plasmonic material, it conducts electric flux density, which generates, detects and manipulates signals in the visible/optical spectrum. Mazin Mustafa from Oklahoma State University notes that meta-materials containing silver can exhibit contradictory behaviours, concluding that silver is able to do two opposing actions.

Black common **Shungite** has a fullerene spin of 20-30 billion RPS (Revolutions per Second), which is expansive and energy giving as well as absorbing negative frequencies two opposing actions happening at the same time.

Silica which is also intelligent (quantum) and conductive at 1 micron thin layers, which is a little known remarkable fact for such an abundant earth element, in black Shungite powder and stones it is around 40-60% of its makeup.

Combining these separately intelligent materials creates an epsilon-negative material (ENM) which is conductive and intelligently capable of selecting appropriate actions for every appliance and person.

A conclusive finding from a study published in 2016 by Science Direct shows that a black C60 Shungite fullerene was more powerful than the C70 Elite stones fullerene. The study found that the 'curvature related spin orbit coupling' in C60 plays a dominant role in the obtained spin-related phenomena because the rugby ball shape of the C70 more commonly found in Elite stones gives it a disadvantage.

Mobile handsets and other devices that have the Oraphim meta-material sticker which has the silver activated powder encapsulated in it produce far less heat from electromagnetic radiation. This is because the frequency is attenuated, and has been reversed by this combination of intelligent materials, the result is a reduction of heat generated by the device which lowers the necrosis effects in the head and hands of the user, as these frequencies are changed from left to right hand spin.

Oraphim guides people to experience these opposing magnetic forces by holding a pair of polished black stones and then a pair with a thin layer of silver activated Shungite powder added to one side followed by an Elite pair. The conducting energy field changes dramatically when people touch the second pair which has the added silver. When people interact with Shungite or Oraphim silver activated (meta-material) product, they often detect both a repelling magnetic field as well as an attracting one, which seems to be due to the diamagnetic repelling effect of the silica combined with the switching effects of the silver to deliver the Shungite quantum energy to clear and unblock energy pathways and systems in the body.

The Shungite is naturally more enhanced with the silver activated powdered layer, and what people are experiencing is the expansion of their own electrical energy 'aura' field being conducted between the stones they are holding and they have to reposition their hands further away as their energy field expands. It's rare to actually experience your own energy field which has people astounded, but it really helps them understand exactly what Shungite is doing for us and our electrical devices.

> *"These stickers are amazing. Feeling the effects already. Devices don't get hot and it may well be a coincidence, but I'm generally feeling better in myself. Awesome! Highly recommend."*
> Rosana 14 Oct, 2022

> *"Can't believe it, but our internet speeds are much faster, and I can now answer my phone at my desk. I could not do that before my Shungite sticker!"*
> Dr H Brew

Shungite's remarkable effectiveness stems from its ability to connect with all living beings and man-made devices through the unseen aether - this invisible medium that interconnects electromagnetic fields (EMFs) from both human and appliance created waves alike. The EMF solutions community is working hard to make these man-made 'aether perturbations' safe, with some companies suggesting blocking these waves via shielding fabrics and Faraday cages. However, Shungite's unique ability to affect the aether on a fundamental level allows it to use and enhance our own 'field' as we have explored; aiding our own body to create a stronger wave that overpowers and influences the direction of negative left spinning man-made EMFs that we encounter in our everyday environment. It's really about seeing what *you* can do to transform your environment with the help of Shungite!

To dive even further in on this topic so that we can take it to a deeper and more personal level of understanding, take a moment to consider that we are all connected as it is often said, but by what? We are actually living within this unseen medium called the aether, this aether transmits these 'wave' like frequencies everywhere, so just imagine for a moment that you are splashing your arms in the swimming pool, you have created a ripple on the surface of the water the 'wave,' but you did not actually add anything new to the water you simply disturbed or 'perturbed' the water, this essentially is what electromagnetic 'waves' are doing, now imagine whizzing this pool of water to spin around you up to the speed of 20-30 billion times a second, and I am sure you will see that this would give some a 'whoosh' feeling of altered frequency about them, and for some to exclaim that their wings are opening, and higher frequencies are indeed being experienced whilst harmful 'waves' are simply overpowered and harmful effects are nullified.

The law of resonance explains that higher frequencies pull lower frequencies up, allowing one's own frequency to alter the mood of a room and others in our lives. Shungite has been measured at 70,000 GHz and still climbing by Walt Silva, we have looked at dowsing as a great way of seeing Shungites effects on the body's outer energy field, and as there are not many measuring devices to track this change in direction (also known as 'attenuation') it's often difficult to measure Shungite's effect and compare it to other modalities. An alternative energy measuring device called the 'Experimental Life Meter' was however used by Derek Condit and he found that Shungite increased his life force energy from 50-60 up to 80 which is a great increase whereas with the Rose Quartz pyramid his energy stayed at 60.

Now just for a moment focus on something that brings you excitement and joy, by creating this frequency you will feel the excitement growing in your heart and belly now, this higher excited feeling will be rippling the aether for others to pick up on affecting the quantum network of your environment; at its core Shungite quantum energy intelligently transforms negative left hand frequencies into positive right hand frequencies for rapid results that cannot be programmed to spin the wrong way, your joy will change the world, and Shungite amplifies this within you as it radiates from you; your joy changes the world.

Section 2

The Wonder Filled World of Water and Shungite Purification

1

Simply - What is Water?

"Water is the rebel element, it won't conform to the laws of physics or gravity and it can't be killed. Without it there is no life. It reincarnates for all to see and science tells us it came to Earth from outer space. Rebellious, nonconformist, eternal and alien.....just look at the power we are filled with."
Veda Austin

We could make assumptions that we are all similarly aware of the unique properties of water, and that we all regard it in the same way, we all use it every day without thinking too much about it on the whole, but it's worth taking a little time to comprehend its unusual qualities in relation to us and our planet.

What exactly is water? "Dare to be naive."
R Buckminster Fuller

It may sound like a daft question, as clearly when water is mentioned we all know what water is! Running and raining down water, frozen floating ice, uplifting steam and fluffy clouds - see it was easy to answer, one element in all its iterations of solid, liquid and gas states or are there others?

Passionate pioneers such as Austrian researcher and inventor Victor Schauberger, Japanese researchers Masaru Emoto followed on by his son, New Zealand artist and researcher Veda Austin, UK scientist Gerald Pollack to name but a few are sharing more of water's beautiful secrets and are each worth a study to surprise you with their findings. With crystalline communications becoming visible as we interact with water, our intentions imprint the water and with new visual hydroglyph responses being captured in the frozen layers with astounding images appearing, Shungite has a quantum message for each of us, a frequency to clear all others, so that we can cleanse on many levels and begin anew, refreshed each day.

Veda Austin's amazing hydroglyphs consistently repeated the same beautiful wave ripples in her frozen water samples, representing 'Creation'. She states *"Fullerene C60 Buckyball passes through two different slits simultaneously, making it the largest particle known to demonstrate the wave/particle duality of matter."*

It is a little known fact that the waters of different oceans do not mix or intermingle as they are distinctly different bodies of water. This begs the question, what really is this water? Perhaps we should approach this topic with a sense of innocence and see what we end up finding and feeling, quite possibly water still has some surprises in store, to instil us with a new sense of awe and wonder, rather than assuming that we already understand the essence of water. Let's start with the assumption that we are all equally unaware and curious about the nature of water and explore this mystery together.

At first glance water may seem like a simple and straightforward substance. However, upon closer inspection it's clear that water is not only a fundamental necessity for life, but it also possesses some mysterious properties. Water's three well known states liquid, vapour and ice have been joined by a fourth state called EZ water. This new state was discovered recently and has the potential to revolutionise the way we think of water.

Dr Gerald Pollack explains that our bodies absorb light from water as an energy source, mimicking the first stages of photosynthesis in plants. Furthermore this EZ water can be used to power electronic devices by utilising infrared light waves, which are free and abundant; Shungite also absorbs the infrared spectrum to perform its water altering tasks. Shungite can create EZ water's hydrophilic action by lowering the surface tension, widening the exclusion zone (EZ) because of its interaction with infrared light frequencies, this is aiding the separating of charged atoms. The ordering of atoms in water forms a crystalline construction like a liquid crystal. The sun's rays are the best source of life giving infrared particles and its exposure is crucial for both our bodies and water, this new EZ water's actual composition is H^2O^3. So water can really power the future in new ways, and in ways that have been suppressed such as the water powered car for instance, Oraphim have even met with a hydrogen / oxygen separating car owner who simply tops up with water and drives away, no nasty emissions or additional costs for fuel taxes to pay, there's no wonder these technologies get suppressed!

Charles Hoy Fort was a researcher whose achievements led to the founding of the 'Aberdeen Fortean Society' and inspired the publication 'Fortean Times'. He spent 27 years cataloguing published facts that did not conform to accepted scientific or academic norms of his time. His four books, published between 1919 and 1932, consist of thousands of strange stories and published experiments that he arranged carefully into categories. These books are filled with astounding reports and articles, including some wild and astonishing accounts of water appearing out of character.

One such account tells the story of a simple brook in the village of Louth (UK) that caused great tragedy one calm day. On the 29th May 1920 with nothing out of the ordinary happening the villagers were going about their daily business as usual, when all of a sudden the River Lud leapt from its banks twenty feet high; an occurrence known as 'a waterspout' with 22 people drowning and 50 houses being devastated. In addition to this Fort's books feature other strange phenomena such as water flowing from ceilings onto furniture. Whilst one may be tempted to dismiss this as a minor inconvenience, it is important to note that the houses of the 1800s had *no* indoor plumbing and it was noted at the time that there was not a cloud in the sky either!

Thanks to YouTube, we now have access to see these 'waterspouts' from 'cloudless skies' as well as some other truly bizarre and fascinating water related phenomena including the movement and levitation via sound frequencies in cymatic experiments. There are certainly many water related mysteries that have yet to be fully explained. Even with our planet being predominantly covered in water to depths beyond our current exploration abilities, we are still discovering new things about it. For example, scientists recently discovered *more* water *beneath* the Earth's crust, which means that textbooks need to be updated on the theoretical composition of our planet. One common misconception is about the tidal movement of water being caused by different moon phases, because it is simply not true that the tides are pulled by the full moon, as water does not contain iron so is not 'magnetic' in that way, so we are left to wonder some more about water its waves and what is happening with the moon above.

Water boils at exactly 100 degrees and freezes at exactly 0 degrees, it reaches the tops of the leaves in the tallest trees and springs magically from the highest mountains defying gravity through its spiralling capillary motion.

Whilst Cassie was studying the fullerene nano structures published in a scientific report the 'Cassie State' was mentioned, which came as a surprise to Cassie from Oraphim. The paper detailed the efficacy of these hydrophilic materials made of fullerenes, and that the 'Cassie State' was written in relation to its 183 degree angle. Interestingly, Cassie from Oraphim has a birthday on the 12th (1+8+3 degree angle = 12), which granted is a tenuous coincidence. However, upon further investigation it was found that this state occurs when water is frozen and air bubbles are formed and it's these frozen bubbles that are called 'Cassie Ice'. Cassie from Oraphim refers to this as 'Quantum Recognition,' which is a connection to our past from a place in the future. Cassie completed her college diploma in Art and Design in the year 2000 and her final exhibition featured macro photography that focused on the tiny bubbles formed in solidified mediums and frozen liquids. The mirror in her life connects her to this vital resource in a moment of quantum entanglement that even had her astonished.

Water is essential to our lives, and with the increasing awareness of its importance, people are searching for safer and purer options for consumption, cooking and bathing. Shungite is proving itself to be a promising solution to this problem as it provides itself as the only everlasting revolutionary solution for water purification in many different ways.

Shungite is widely used in Russia as the best alternative to charcoal for water treatment. It has the ability to blast apart chemicals and it outperforms its carbon counterpart many times over. The best part is that it *never* needs to be replaced due to its *unique* properties.

Unlike traditional carbon filters that absorb chemicals to a lesser efficacy depending on the make, and are generally expensive and not recyclable, Shungite with a one time purchase has a unique ability to reverse the molecular spin of chemicals at speeds of 20-30 billion times per second causing their nullification.

Oleg Mosin from the Moscow State University of Applied Biotechnology, Ignat Ignatov from the Scientific Research Centre of Medical Biophysics and the University in Sofia, Bulgaria published the following information covering common water pollutants and Shungite removal rates:

Common Water Pollutants	**Removal Degree %**
Iron Fe^{2+}/Fe^{3+}	95
Zinc Zn^{2+}	80
Lead Pb^{2+}	85
Copper Cu^{2+}	85
Carbon Disulphide Cs^{2+} a colourless, toxic, highly volatile and flammable liquid chemical compound, large amounts of which are used in the manufacture of viscose rayon, cellophane	90
Strontium St^{2+} High levels of radioactive strontium can damage bone marrow and cause anaemia and prevent the blood from clotting properly	97
Radionuclides: Radioactive forms of elements are called radionuclides	90

Fluorine: Fluorine gas is very irritating and very dangerous to the eyes, skin and lungs. Fluorine gas at low concentrations makes your eyes and nose hurt. At higher concentrations it becomes hard to breathe. Exposure to high concentrations of fluorine can cause death due to lung damage	80
Ammonia: Ammonia is a colourless highly irritating gas with a sharp suffocating odour. It dissolves easily in water to form ammonium hydroxide solution which can cause irritation and burns	90
Chlorine and organochlorine compounds: Chlorinated hydrocarbon (CHC) is a generic term given to compounds containing chlorine, carbon and hydrogen. The term can be used to describe organochlorine pesticides such as lindane and DDT, industrial chemicals such as polychlorinated biphenyls (PCB), and chlorine waste products such as dioxins and furans	95
Phenols: Exposure to phenol may cause irritation to the skin, eyes, nose, throat and nervous system. Some symptoms of exposure to phenol are weight loss, weakness, exhaustion, muscle aches and pain. Severe exposure can cause liver and/or kidney damage, skin burns, tremor, convulsions and twitching	90

Dioxins: Short term exposure of humans to high levels of dioxins may result in skin lesions, such as chloracne and patchy darkening of the skin and altered liver function. Long term exposure is linked to impairment of the immune system, the developing nervous system, the endocrine system and reproductive functions. Dioxins can also potentially contaminate fruits and vegetables by being deposited with airborne particles (dust) on plant surfaces or directly from contact with contaminated soil. Dioxins can pass into aquatic organisms and eventually find their way into the food chain. (Suggestion: wash fruit and vegetables in Shungite water)	97
Helminths' eggs: Adult worms live in the intestine where they produce thousands of eggs each day. In areas that lack adequate sanitation, these eggs contaminate the soil	90
Smell	85
Turbidity: Turbidity is the measure of relative clarity of a liquid. It is an optical characteristic of water and is a measurement of the amount of light that is scattered by material in the water when a light is shone through the water sample	95

In October 2020 the Journal of Water Chemistry and Technology published a substantial study of Shungite's effects on water. This study conducted by L A Deremeshko, M N Balakina and D D Kucheruk yielded many impressive results.

- Shungite demonstrated a disinfecting effect when used as a half-cell of the galvanic couple; removing coliform bacteria from treated water.

- The oxidation reduction (redox) potential was reduced from 340 mV to 255 mV; which is noteworthy since this parameter is considered one of the most important parameters of water in its interaction with the human body.

- In addition the study examined the impact of Shungite on the toxin load of fluoride. When tested on water with a fluoride content of 9.1 mg/dm3 from Mashevka and Poltava Oblast regions in the Ukraine Shungite was highly effective at decreasing the fluoride ion content of the treated water from 9.1 mg/dm3 to 0.9 mg/dm3 in just 5 minutes.

Oraphim invested in the Palintest Photometer 7500 which is a high end water analysis equipment; and Shungite astonished all by showing its instantaneous rapid purifying action. They were already aware that Shungite could behave in unconventional ways and with clues from research pointing to the fact that it can break molecular bonds and not be absorbing the toxins, they wanted to find a way which would result in altering the chemical composition of the samples without the contact of the Shungite in the water itself, they devised an experiment that captured something truly remarkable on a quantum level.

By deciding to use the toggle and a Shungite sticker on the *outside* of the test tube there could not be any possibility of contaminating the water sample with any of the minerals contained in the Shungite, as this would also not add anything else to the water either.

The results were visible, the tap water turned yellow because the chlorine that was present reacted to the potassium iodide in the acid solution which releases the iodine, yet *all* the Shungite samples remained crystal clear for 5 days whether the Shungite had physically touched the water or *not*, leading to the conclusion that Shungite worked instantaneously both in contact with the water and without directly touching; this was proving that toggles work to nullify the chlorine when placed on taps and bottles.

Cassie placed the test tubes to one side and there was another surprise that the Shungite wanted to show, as five days later the clear Shungite samples began to yellow, and ten days later they matched the original tap water sample, revealing that the chlorine had been there all along, but the chemical bonds had indeed been broken by the effect of the Shungite energy, exactly the same as the water that the Shungite ran over momentarily, and as the energy must have slowed or dissipated the chlorine bonds had reformed, a full five days of purified water, from a moments touch of Shungite energy.

The fluoride experiments were performed in a similar manner, with visible results identifying the clearly contaminated tap water from the purified Shungite water. Testing for fluoride requires an acid solution with Zirconyl Chloride and Eriochrome Cyanine R to form the red colour; the presence of fluoride will degrade this red and turn it orange.

Free full colour picture resources available at
www.shungiteexpectmiracles.me

QUANTUM PURIFICATION

Molecular bonds of toxic chemicals are broken by the Shungite energy.
Toxic chemicals rotation is opposite to the way our cells rotate. -Walt Silva

Fluoride nullified with Shungite

The darkest red of all the samples

Distilled Water | Elite & black Shungite | 15 Stage Filter | Tap water

The darker the Red the less Fluoride present

When chlorine is present the water sample turns yellow because the chlorine reacts with potassium iodide in the acid solution
(Water purity: iodine release method)

The water samples remained purified of chlorine for 5 days with both options:
the toggle or sticker on the outside or in contact by touching the stones for 1 second

Crystal clear

Yellow

5 Days Later — Yellow Yellow Yellow

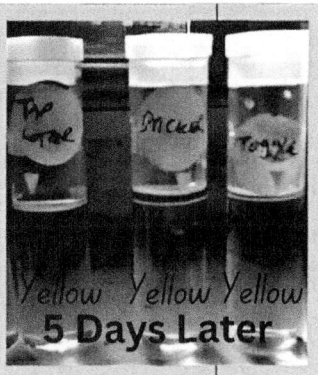

Shungite stones can be used in the bath and shower heads to clear Chlorine which has a negative impact on our healthy ingestion and processing of nutrients. Chlorine inhibits the sulphur in our foods from being processed and our bloodstream from being activated with oxygenated blood. This is detrimental to our cells which need energy to complete their life cycle and not mutate and multiply as cancer cells. It is vital that our cells receive enough energy to perform 'apoptosis' also known as 'programmed cell death' otherwise these die-eased cells can clump together forming cancerous masses.

Shungite is the only available element that when used in the last stages of filtration is capable of clearing the water of hazardous medical substances such as pharmaceutical medicines from the water supply according to Yuri Klavdievich, a Doctor of Technical Sciences.

Studies conducted by M V Kopylov, I N Bolgova, N L Kleymenova concluded that Shungite's influence on water is diverse. During the process of water purification it acts as a filtering material, sorbent, catalyst of purification and reduction processes and as a biological disinfection agent in the purification of industrial waste filtering processes of the heavily polluting petrochemical industry.

Shungite is so amazing that it can even affect the aether and water in a container without physically touching it, which is often overlooked by mainstream examiners and scientists on the topic.

Shungite instantly lowers the surface tension in water, which is a key element for proper healthy hydration. With Shungite it's about the quality of your drinking water, not the quantity. The cells in our bodies do not easily absorb poor quality water molecules so that most who are drinking 'recommended' levels of water (up to two litres a day) are simply flooding their system, flushing out their electrolytes and yet they remain still chronically dehydrated as discussed by Dr R Cywes, but the transformed Shungite water is accepted easily and highly absorbed by our cells resulting in the requirement for much smaller volumes of water to hydrate fully and completely each day.

Dr Patrick Flanagan, an inventor with over 300 patents to his name conducted water research and studies, and his findings revealed similarities in drinking water among remote civilisations that experienced longevity, the common denominator was lowered surface tension. Shungite has the ability to instantly lower surface tension resulting in better hydration of the body's cells, increased nutrient uptake and importantly the effective removal of waste materials. Regardless of your location whether you're in the city, rural areas, or remote locations Shungite transformed water can provide life giving hydration and vital detoxification unlike any other water purification method available.

There are various studies examining healthy water options which highlight results that show that when water molecules move around in a much more ordered manner that this is highly beneficial, this is called a 'liquid crystal' state by Russian Scientist S V Shirinkin, and we can guess that Shungite will be doing this too as its negative ions are put into an ordered state due to the lowered surface tension, as well as Shungite water having a lower freezing point and even capturing what are called 'Cassie ice' bubbles in toroidal spirals when frozen. With the additional fullerenes hydrating the water molecules exactly so that they fit perfectly inside the icosahedral water cluster acting as an excellent stabiliser, explains Shirinkin.

Anything within Shungite's hydrogen rich liquid crystal water is potentially free from oxidation which is why Shungite was used to stop boats from rusting by the Russian Navy. On top of that Professor Andrevski's discovery that the fullerenes neutralise the free radicals and uses its components to build more complex structures unlike vitamin C, Shungite which gives up its donor electrons to neutralise them safely, making Shungite a compound that is a stronger detoxification agent and its effects last longer to detoxify us safely.

The restructuring process of Shungite water is done at a very rapid rate, which is also known as the 'kinetic electric effect.' This is what gives Shungite water its softer taste and better cleaning ability. Shungite water performs a very clever ion exchange, so your essential minerals are left safely in your cells, but the damaging crud, spent heavy metals and free radicals are removed safely from the body's cells in the fullerenes which are small enough to be expelled in our urine.

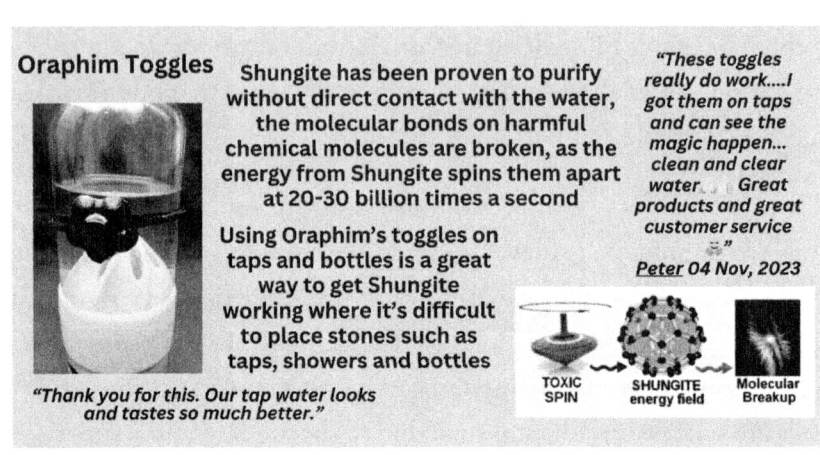

Oraphim Toggles

Shungite has been proven to purify without direct contact with the water, the molecular bonds on harmful chemical molecules are broken, as the energy from Shungite spins them apart at 20-30 billion times a second

Using Oraphim's toggles on taps and bottles is a great way to get Shungite working where it's difficult to place stones such as taps, showers and bottles

"Thank you for this. Our tap water looks and tastes so much better."

"These toggles really do work....I got them on taps and can see the magic happen... clean and clear water. Great products and great customer service 😊"

Peter 04 Nov, 2023

TOXIC SPIN | SHUNGITE energy field | Molecular Breakup

Does Shungite alter the pH level of water? Some websites have made claims that it does increase the pH to sell their pH altering / alkalising equipment explains Nancy L Hopkins in her defence of Shungite, so Oraphim have tried a number of different methods to ascertain some clarity on the topic and double check for themselves. For the first test they purchased litmus paper and the colour of the paper remained the same, in the second test for pH they used 15 in 1 water analysis test strips, both options are easily available and affordable on major selling platforms, and it's a lot of fun trying your own water testing experiments.

Comparing four water samples of Doncaster tap water, their baseline pH reading was 6.2, the use of a 15 stage filter, black and elite Shungite samples and the results showed that there was a momentary increase in pH with the black Shungite sample going from 6.2 to 6.8, although the 15 stage filter sample had risen to 8.4, the Elite sample had stayed at 6.2, the test was repeated less than 2 minutes later and the two Shungite samples were now the same 6.2 which was the same as the original Doncaster tap water sample.

Other measurements showed that the instant effects on the water from both of the two types of Shungite had lowered the hardness, nitrates, fluoride and the alkalinity was '0'.

These results were much more favourable than the 15 stage filter tested alongside the Shungite, which is very encouraging indeed, and a true testament that Shungite works instantly to turn water into the elixir for all life to benefit without having to wait around for too long at all; with Elite stones only fractionally faster than the common and cheaper black Shungite.

Dr Adam D Wexler makes some astounding points from his research with water and electricity; which essentially is every single drop of seawater on the planet due to its electrolyte salt content and to bring it home every single drop of the 100,000,000,000,000,000,000,000 (100 sextillion) drops of water in the average human body. Out of all these drops there are top surfing protons emerging from the multitude of normal water cells, these are positively charged hydrogen and they surf around searching at supersonic speeds connecting to others that are similarly charged special hydrogen particles. This highlights our need for connection, searching each other out, our nature mirrored on a molecular level and its highlighting our longing to unify and make connections with one another which is fundamental to us as beings of water.

As each water molecule needs to connect it is a reflection of one we experience on our internal micro scale and also externally on a macro scale in day to day life. What is interesting to examine alongside this phenomena is the microscopic photos of of water droplets inside the Bosnian pyramids that have the tiny escaping mystery elements that when placed alongside pictures of 'orbs' they match exactly as they are identical, is it that 'orbs' are in fact these very same 'surfing' positively charged hydrogen particles?

With all that water in the body did you know that the human eye is made up of a total of 98% water, with the majority of it being the aptly named aqueous and vitreous humor? Now when you look in the mirror what do you see; do you see the spirit of water?

We cannot be parted from water for any time at all, it belongs in us and us in it, with our eyes we well up with pain and joy, we see all that is to be judged through these eyes that can be open or closed to seeing the wonder and kindness as well as immense evil and cruelty that is abundant here on Earth.

A collection of creative flowings and writings on water by Cassie:

Polluted mind, body and souls

We pay the highest price

to pump this chemical liquid,

Poisoned water,

It is passed through people,

Who have been pissed up,

Pissed off and pissed on,

Left without a pot to piss in!

God is here, God is everywhere, could it be that God is simply the water within us,

Pure beautiful crystal thirst quenching, life giving water,

could this be why ungodly governments poison this gracious resource?

I thank God for there being water, of course.

What is water, what is me?

Water is the mighty raging sea but so is the drizzle as gentle as can be

Mesmerising as a stream flowing and frosty as the fresh snow snowing.

Defying gravity ice floats by, melting glaciers into little glasses together we rise high

We sip, gargle, steam and swallow, liquefying solids which float up to our brain

The molecules of excitement falling down magically as rain

It sees you smile and connects all our very vital parts,

Yet each droplet remembers your every thought and beats in all our hearts,

Your worries and desires your past your present and future

Your spirit entwined with water - do we hear it's calling from where we once began

It infuses your dreams and awakens your soul for you in me for now forever.

From it you were flushed, from wherein it you grew and lived

Waters was once your home, 9 months where you began it

Now, it's still within you - do you see your reflection in it?

Be born once more into its flowing embrace

As it cleans your body and helps win every race

Without it we are nothing, just simply empty space.

Family Reflections: I sea an ocean of possibilities in you

The sea waves and beckons us closer to a far distant destination, as children we ran into the ebb and flow of life's rocky seas from the same internal waters we seven were birthed from our motherland yet fashioned from different captains, a crew of 11 odd bods I am connected to each of you somehow, somewhere…..still, in my mind you dwell.

We rain independently at last, as we embark with our future before us, done looking to the past, with squally storms on the horizon, we once did sail together, gone are the days of growing, we fled and jumped or fell from the mother crow's nest. For some of my siblings they landed unsure of themselves, they crowed and flapped, now we all wept tears for times to come and those gone by, as our family was broken before it was ever made, a mirror reflecting the whole body of society.

Each man an island surrounded by what they perceive or perturbed by each day anew ending and beginning for us all an expanse of calm sea as flat as a sheet of paper to write the wrongs and sing the songs of the souls parting waves, we sailed on, away me hearties, each steers a new uncharted course, 19 C_vid pirates will ravage our lives, setting sails and churning waters of unsaid emotions grace and bounty both were lost, my bough is stern, my treasures and pains remain a mystery, my course corrected and each made a choice to set compass on a star bound trajectory, each soul a vital drop in the ocean of humanities dream, I remember you dearly my darlings each seafaring siblings sweet smile, out there you are, yet still you remain in my heart.

The purest water can heal the toughest conditions, gentle water wears down the hardest stone and flows to where it is needed internally and externally, all we have to do is clean *it* so it can clean *us*, it detoxes us and leads us in ways that we have not perceived before.

Can we truly answer the question, what is water?; or what are we? Are we a separate entity to it, possibly not and its connection to Shungite is truly transformational and magical and the same can be said about you.

2

Imitating Nature: Water Purification and Distillation

Nowadays there are so many different purifying water methods all working to different degrees, it can be as simple as using a stick as a filter as shown in survival videos or purchasing tabletop filters and inline sink reverse osmosis options. Some people opt for expensive electrical devices that pass water over metal plates with electrical currents, these include devices like the Kangen water systems, unfortunately this type of device negatively affects the water as the metals oxidise and this causes chlorine to form in the water unknowingly to its users as explained and demonstrated by former Kangen saleslady Amanda Bobbett.

On the other hand simple carbon filters are expensive to continually replace and reported to be only 10% effective, as we have tested earlier with a slightly more complicated 15 stage filter that was used as a comparison to Shungite and it has not done the job Shungite can do. The chemicals were still present, and with the filter not being recyclable it's not really a good option after all, and it did leave the tap water similar to how it started with no life or frequency added or altered. Similarly 'reverse osmosis' does not change the frequency of the water either and removes beneficial and vital minerals and then there are the extremely costly but well packaged and marketed solutions that offer no water purification at all, and could just be expensive 'structuring' gimmicks at an eye watering price, Oraphim believe that having access to health solutions should not be exclusively available for the richer among us.

It is essential to understand that water has memory and is programmed by the frequencies of chemicals, minerals, other bodies it has travelled through as well as mechanical processing and our thoughts. Therefore to fully purify water on all levels water requires:

- Memory clearing process
- Remineralisation
- Re-energising
- Restructured, from being in deadened pipe systems
- Nullification or removal of chemicals
- Microorganisms and microflora removal so we don't become ill
- Turbidity, clarity of the water
- Lowered surface tension for hydration
- We need to make it taste nice too!

One popular option is distillation which removes 100% of the particles and impurities in water, just like in nature with the cycles of water turning into vapour, forming clouds and raining, this process changes the water, which is now cleansed, pure and post distillation it is 'magnetic' with fresh new abilities to attract the negative ions which it was not able to before in its vapour stage.

With rainwater created through this natural process of distillation, these 'ionic magnetic' raindrops attract pollution particles in the sky created by industry and modern living which is why we get the 'fresh' feeling after a downpour. Distilled water is favoured by window cleaners for this 'magnetic effect' that leaves windows perfectly clean and streak free because each drop is attracting the ions in the dirt into the water during the cleaning. Distilled water can cleanse on many levels, including the spiritual level, making it great for 'spooky' houses as well as for dirty windows.

- 'Magnetic' distilled water requires reprogramming with new frequencies and remineralising to mimic nature's soil remineralisation and swirling streams for reprogramming.

- Victor Schauberger stated that distillation of water for creating healthy drinking water is only half the process, with the adding of minerals and movement for the restructuring for a period of up to 24 hours is ideally required for the completion of the cycle.

- Dr Mercola's report on distilled water covered the study of 3000 people all using distilled water; all 3000 of them had mineral deficiency due to the 'magnetic' effect of distilled water as the distilled water was pulling *all* minerals from the cells. The article also explained that distilled water is acidic, and the body pulls calcium from the bones to create protection for the vital organs from this acidic water.

Looking back at nature's processes, our rainwater is reprogrammed, restructured and remineralised by filtering through the earth, emerging and swirling over pebbles to create the best healthy life giving water; reproducing this complete process from the tap / rain water we have available to us as best we can makes total sense.

Oraphim stones sourced from Zazhoginskoje are known for their healing properties. To ensure that the stones are free from any contaminants that may have entered during the mining and packaging process Oraphim give them a thorough washing before packaging, it's recommended to use just a few Shungite plain stone chips together, three together creates a coherent field and one on its own would be lonely and energetically not as active.

To prepare:

- Simply rinse the stones under a tap to remove any recent dust and add them to a jug.

- The longer you let the stones infuse the water before drinking the more energising and delicious it becomes.

- Be mindful about drinking it before bedtime as the energising effect may keep you awake. Instead it's best to decant enough for your night time drink and enjoy the revitalising energy every morning and during the day.

- The use of Shungite is safe for long term use with no adverse effects.

- It's important to be a little cautious when using the stones and not to overdo it by adding too many stones to a small amount of water; simply remember that three stones can be enough. Using more stones than necessary in a small amount of water may result in a strong cleaning, purging effect.

- This is testament to just how effective Shungite really is as often reports of 100 gms per 1 litre is cited, but in Oraphim's experience this is much *too* much and only three small stones are actually needed.

- With simple Shungite steam inhalation for chronic obstructive pulmonary disease (COPD), which is said to be caused by mould spores in the lungs. COPD requires the need of an antifungal, which Shungite is, in this way Shungite vapour is delivering KELEA life force activated fullerene rich healing water vapour to places that drinking water cannot reach killing the mould spores in the lungs, with many people getting rapid relief and being able to radically reduce the use of inhalers. Pollen allergies can be treated in the same way.

The toggles are easy to attach to hoses, taps and bottles, making the water transformation process simple when it is more difficult to use stones. Shungite is so amazing that it does not even need to touch the water to affect it, as its quantum connecting energy creates transformations for its ability to give delicious and healing water through the sides of any and all containers.

In Thorne, Doncaster, a group have been meeting for a few years, sharing concerns over the quality of their tap water they decided to do a taste test by bringing in samples from eight different regions, covering about sixty miles and taste each one in turn. After grading each sample for taste they added Shungite and tasted them again. To their delight and surprise, every single sample had greatly improved in taste in a very short space of time. Another great example you can try with your friends and family: have a water tasting Shungite experiment too; or just notice how children and animals easily find Shungite water much more desirable to drink than untreated tap water.

The Karelia region is home to some of the world's largest and most breathtaking lakes. For example Lake Baikal holds 5% of all the freshwater on the Earth's surface. One of the unique features of these lakes is the purity of the water which is safe for drinking directly from the lakes without any filtration.

Shungite is a natural and safe solution that can help to improve and maintain your overall health enhancing the most vital element that we take in - water, for our spirits long term survival in our human bodies. Without it we do not get to stay on Earth very long and yet it is poisoned, polluted and perturbed, and our connection to it is often overlooked as many turn to mixing flavourings to make it passable with diluted colourful chemical squashes added to it to make the already poisoned water palatable.

Oraphim received a photo of a lady's distiller; she had been filling with water that had been 'Shungited' by the Oraphim toggle that was on her tap. The water distilled, and she repeated this process and was amazed to find a perfect six sided hexagon in the crud deposit at the base of the distiller. Oraphim has reproduced the same hexagonal deposit using a Shungite toggle on their tap used for filling up a distiller and finds this a fascinating way to show the perfect geometry that Shungite is producing in its water, because it has programmed the tap water. This is also known as restructuring, and the hexagon is one of the constituent shapes of the fullerene. Shungite is always finding ways to communicate it's abilities to us!

Imitating Nature: Water Purification and Distillation | **115**

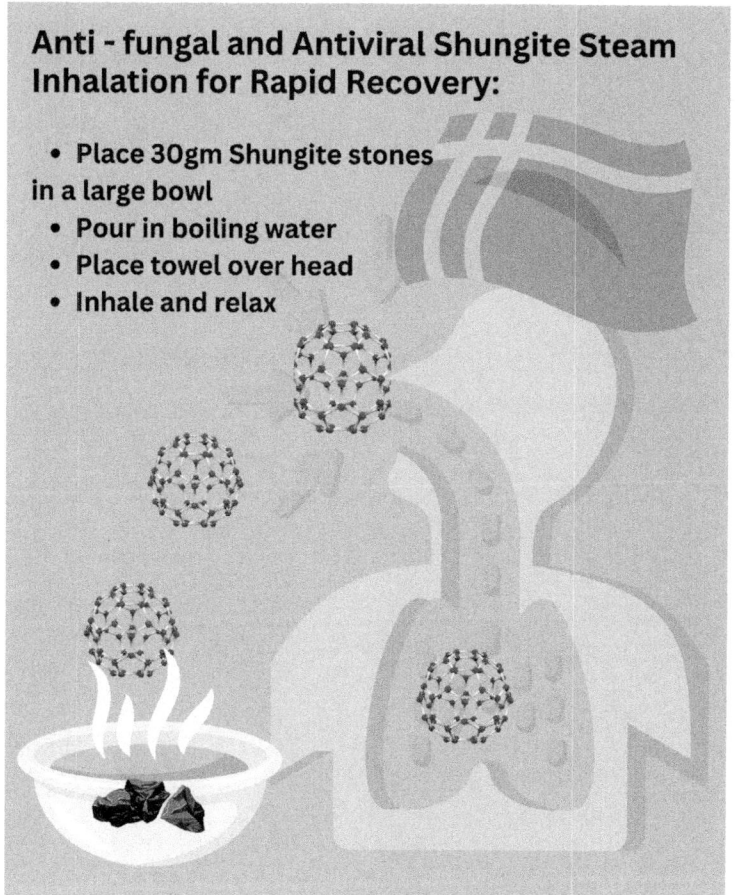

Anti - fungal and Antiviral Shungite Steam Inhalation for Rapid Recovery:

- Place 30gm Shungite stones in a large bowl
  - Pour in boiling water
  - Place towel over head
  - Inhale and relax

3

Radioactive Toxic Water Clean Up

"Treated carbon (shungite) pulls radioactive elements from water" An extraordinary scientific discovery by Rice and Kazan University has proven that Shungite removes radioactive particles strontium and caesium from water.

Researchers at Rice University and Kazan Federal University in Russia have formulated a one-of-a-kind sorbent from Shungite capable of extracting radioactive particles from water; the discovery is paramount in purifying the hundreds of millions of gallons of contaminated water retained after the Fukushima nuclear plant accident. The compound developed by the researchers is cost effective and highly efficient at absorbing radioactive caesium and strontium. These toxic elements were released into the environment when the Fukushima plant experienced a meltdown after a strange earthquake and tsunami in March 2011. Tour, a Rice chemist, who led the project with Ayrat Dimiev, a former post-doctoral researcher, in his laboratory and now a research professor revealed that their compound can easily trap common radioactive elements found in water floods from oil extraction, including uranium, thorium and radium.

The two variations of OMC particles – one from coke derived carbon and the other from Shungite – have a crumpled paper ball or rose like appearance with highly irregular petals. The researchers tested them by mixing the sorbents with contaminated water as well as through column filtration; a standard process in which fluid is pumped or pulled by gravity through a filter to remove contaminants. OMC2 (from Shungite) in the same concentrations adsorbed 70 percent of caesium and 47 percent of strontium. The researchers were surprised to see that plain Shungite particles extracted almost as much caesium as its oxidised counterpart; Dimiev noted *"Interestingly, plain Shungite was used by local people for water purification from ancient times. But we have increased its efficiency many times, as well as revealed the factors behind its effectiveness."*

Carbon presents a distinct advantage over other materials used for remediation of radioactive waste as it can be burned in a nuclear incinerator leaving only a small amount of radioactive ash that's much easier to store. *"Just passing contaminated water through OMC filters will extract the radioactive elements and permit safe discharge to the ocean"* Tour said *"This could be a major advance for the clean-up effort at Fukushima."* he concluded.

In a separate study by Professor A Sosyukin of over 500 patients with different conditions at a Military Medical Academy reported that his patients with acute poisoning from the Chernobyl accident had an increase in immune function from their use of Shungite.

An inexplicable radiation leak on the outskirts of Doncaster was detected in 2022 towards the more rural town of Thorne strangely coinciding with the rupturing of the surface of a back country road surrounded by fields, which meant that it had to be closed for complete repair, a local lady was having a telephone session with a medium who reported to her client that there was radiation in her vicinity unknowing that indeed there was, the lady purchased an Oraphim Shungite pendant and this solved the immediate radiation issue for the client to great relief as the clairvoyant confirmed on subsequent sessions.

Travelling Abroad: Pamela was completely baffled when she was asked to step aside for additional scanning at airport security, she had already taken off all that would set off their scanners, the security personnel said that there were 'orange patches' showing up on the X-ray scans (X-rays being radiation, so best to avoid if possible). Whilst discussing this with Cassie who had heard of similar occurrences where Shungite bead bracelets had left an orange patch on the body showing up on similar airport X-ray scans, Pamela made the connection, she had put the Shungite deodorant on that morning and that was where the scanners were detecting something - the orange patches, because Pamela had also used the deodorant as a perfume bar adding a little extra protection in other places around the body!

Shungite is here with its ability to clear up our toxic environment, and it's great to be able to report that it has already started, the macro and the micro, each of us on a personal mission to clean up on many levels emotionally, physically as well as our environment too.

4

Capturing the Quantum - Shungite Surprises

Shungite is proven to break toxic chemical bonds rendering them harmless as they pass through the body and this is an important factor in educating people about the benefits of using it. A particular concern that Oraphim was often asked about was the chlorine and fluoride, that was why Cassie decided to focus on these two. Shungite energy instantly broke the chlorine bonds, improving water quality for up to five days; there was no active chlorine present to inhibit our normal biological functions. Through Oraphim's water analysis equipment they were able to confirm this phenomenon, and within the time of making a cup of tea they were watching as the experiment revealed its quantum reaction. These groundbreaking research results were conducted by artist Cassie who has a passion to help others understand the fundamental nature of Shungite.

Shungite energy is fundamentally spinning elements to be nullified or beneficial to life. To the unwitting eye it may appear as though Shungite increases negative elements, when only reading the numbers that appear on apparatus, in fact, it is instantly breaking their bonds which is why it appears to create more chlorine molecules when it is in fact nullifying them. When the Shungite toggle or sticker is not in direct contact with the water sample, it is not able to increase negative elements but instead causes molecular break up, as shown in Nancy L Hopkins book 'Shungite the Study of Energy.'

The proto-energy from the quantum field structures water's frequency, accessing our realm through each Shungite stone or particle of dust from Shungite, eliminating distortions or disturbance from the negative effects of chemicals. The body seems not to be disturbed by any potential harm from toxins or minerals in the water but instead cells are given access only to the beneficial frequencies of each mineral that is required.

When scientists are conducting experiments looking at Shungite in a laboratory they generally employ a standard methodology using the stones in the water; they see and report their results but this is not the whole story. This leads to assumptions about their results without understanding a much bigger picture and they have missed what has actually happened to the water, they lack understanding regarding the nature of the torsion spin-field physics which allows the fullerene molecule to access missing mineral frequencies which means that there is a misunderstanding about what is occurring when the body is being 'remineralised', repaired and supported by Shungite energy infused water.

Oraphim were able to capture this quantum story by analysing Shungite's effects alongside other water purification methods, such as a 15 stage filter, by using Shungite on the *outside* of the container which is highly unconventional, this a quantum reaction which can be captured if you know what to look out for.

Magan Tyson wrote a testimonial on Cosmic Reality after listening to a podcast by Nancy L Hopkins "Dear Nancy and all: Listened to Shungite Radio when you talked about putting Shungite nuggets on water pipes. Well I put one Oraphim Shungite sticker (silver activated) on my cold water pipe and like you said no chlorine smell and softer water and better suds in the water when washing pots etc., my neighbours are witnessing the same reaction" she concludes "I have covered 6 flats and I am well impressed and with other household electrical items like you explain that there is a 20% + in electrical reduction etc…"

It was similar feedback from the placing of our Shungite stickers on the water in-pipe on a washing machine that inspired Cassie to invent the toggles. She pondered: *if the water is softer this will make the suds more foamy - the Shungite is able to work without physically being in contact with the water, and this reaction in the water is happening instantaneously too.*

One man reported that the temperature on his boiler had risen by a full 12 degrees by simply adding an Oraphim Toggle to the tap. He was able to alter the heat settings so that he got the same hot water as before, using much less fuel to fire up his boiler, but that also his cold tap had got colder!

Tina reported back that the toggle on her shower has changed the frequency she had to clean the scale deposits from the shower head, before the toggle it needed cleaning in vinegar every two weeks and she has not had to clean it yet and it's been three months.

Water Transformer Toggles reviews:

"I had staph infection in my nose for months. In the end I took antibiotics as it wasn't shifting it went then returned. I went to doctor Saturday morning started drinking the water, by Sat evening I noticed my nose was healing rapidly no other explanation other than the Shungite Toggle!" Zoe

"This is an excellent invention!"

"Fantastic, absolutely love how these work. Great product and speedy delivery. Many thanks!"

"Put this around my water bottle for purification and detox. My skin looks better don't know if it's the benefit but will continue to drink and keep you posted. Thanks again. X"

"Great product! I have one around all my water bottles and I also use one as my hair tie! Thank you so much!"

"Thank you for this. Our tap water looks and tastes so much better."

"I've used the Shungite in the bath and that blew me away I always have sea salt baths and I added the Shungite to the bath water in the little bag I've never felt anything like the difference in the water quality it actually felt as if the water had changed it had a different consistency with it more silky consistency and I have to say having come out of the bath I feel amazing calm peaceful serene happy and so cleansed it's a cleansing I've never felt before or experienced"

5

Homoeopathy and Quantum States of Healing

"The day science begins to study non-physical phenomena; it will make more progress in one decade than all the previous centuries of its existence"
Nicola Tesla

Shungite was employed in a study to test its efficacy using a homoeopathic approach, where the frequency of Shungite was taken and used instead of working in a direct contact way with the Shungite stones, with great results too, as it's all about frequency imprinting and healing.

Shungite has been found to be effective in similar ways to Dr Bach's flower remedies and even stronger Australian plant and flower versions. The homoeopathic water samples measured 'KELEA', which is the equivalent to the 'life energy' force proposed by others and variously called chi, prana, orgone, etc. KELEA activated water has been shown to positively impact many dire health conditions, especially those in which the metabolism of food is impaired. This can result from insufficient oxygen because of diseases such as impaired blood supply from cardiovascular and cerebrovascular diseases and metabolic derangements. For example certain conditions require additional oxygen molecules to be delivered such as in diabetes, malnutrition and increased energy demands as in infections and during tissue repair; Shungite's abilities to deliver the needed energy is having a remarkable effect for many patients covering a wide range of conditions.

Being saturated in cellularly matching frequencies from healing tones of music to living in harmonised environments can be major contributing factors to our well being, this is the conclusion from recent advances in quantum biology. Shungite can harmonise our environment and also the water so we become harmonised within and around us, the more we can do to live in a state of complete coherence, as a state of order of matter, coupled with electromagnetic (EM) fields will put us at ease and not in a state of dis-ease. Coherent phenomena are well explained by quantum field theory (QFT), a well-established theoretical framework in quantum physics.

Water as we know is essential for life, being the medium used by living organisms to carry out various biochemical reactions and playing a fundamental role in coherent phenomena; to have Shungite enhancing our water with quantum energy is very special as it does indeed become a very magical elixir for life that also connects us to our outer environment.

Our bodies can reveal many more insights about us when we see things going wrong, much more than we think. Chris Thomas and Diane Baker's book 'Everything You Always Wanted to Know About Your Body, But So Far Nobody's Been Able to Tell You' is a comprehensive guide to mind-body medicine that links the frequency of energy centres in the body to debilitating diseases and the mind states of the individual. They discuss natural medicines and resonance healing herbs and modalities which have been a fascinating companion for Cassie to study medical, mind and emotional mapping of the body's responses to thoughts and behaviours.

Ernest Rossi's 'The Psychobiology of Mind-Body Healing' delves into these concepts in an even deeper way with his synthesises and findings in the field of mind-body healing across various disciplines and time. This is all about the sympathetic resonance of our thoughts and our body's cells working together, 'dis-ease' can simply be when we have shifted out of alignment, a thought correction is a frequency shift that can correct the environment in the body to come back into wellness.

Professor Andrievsky explains that "Shungite fullerenes act on a systemic level and not as a treatment for an illness." To help us 'get better' we need to understand where our illnesses come from, we need to consider that they may have started energetically from within us at some point.

Changing our own minds can be the biggest hurdle that we can encounter sometimes, but it's the key to everything else moving into alignment, altering the thought or response alters the frequency which is a way to prevent dis-ease manifesting into debilitating conditions that affects us physically and can be achieved (if we want it to be this way).

The ability to match the healing environments together, simply giving the body the most beneficial water possible or altering the body's water content by wearing Shungite alters the environment for the cells to thrive. The latest independent research carried out with live blood analysis by Philip showed that in the presence of silver activated Shungite blood cells lived twice as long before they break down.

The water within us is activated when we hear coherent frequencies such as musical notes played in particular healing tunings, Rich naturally tunes his guitar in a very rare and unconventional way, the outcome is that every note played is in complete sympathetic resonance naturally with every cell in our body. The listener not only hears the music but also feels it deeply within because the special tunings are not the modern A = 440 Hz. Modern changes in musical tunings were brought about by the Rockefeller and Carnegie Foundations in the 1940s, there was much resistance from musicians worldwide (traditionally A was 432 Hz which is coherent).

The patterns that sound vibrations create are called 'cymatics', these are beautifully complete formed patterns. When the correct frequency is played something magical happens, a whole world of potential unlocks nodes of information in the aether, but not when out of tune or out of coherence music is played. Cassie was witness to a wonderful moment once when Rich was playing his guitar, it was snowing outside and as Rich began to play the snow whirled and danced and as he stopped so did the snow stop its dancing too and it just fell as normal.

What was the real reason behind changing the concert pitch A from 432 Hz to 440 Hz by the Rockefeller and Carnegie foundations?

Oraphim have had lots of fun teaching these concepts at various events using tone generators, speakers, sand and pioneering water marbling techniques; the patterns become alive when the node of information in the frequency is activated. When you access particular states of frequency within your being, your mind can receive new information from the 'Field', often this is in the daydreaming state or when listening to music that is cellularly coherent which Rich is becoming more called to perform more than ever before, so we should be listening to healing tuned musicians and encouraged to daydream more!

Frequency disturbances that can disable a person during a traumatic stroke event have been shown to be successfully alleviated very rapidly in some instances, explains Norman Doidge in his accounts of miraculous recoveries involving stroke patients. He details accounts of patients after serious accidents involving trauma to the head, explaining that there is an energy transfer into the body, which can disrupt the inner workings.

Cassie was working as a carer when her client suffered a stroke, so she utilised a Shungite pyramid as well as implementing his techniques for brain remapping, these tools and techniques rapidly altered her client, which was a great relief for her and her family, as they could instantly see how their mothers disposition returned to her pre-stroke self, with brain remapping techniques to instantly aid the client's ability to begin beautiful flowing coordination in her walking after just a few tiny movements of her client's nose. With subtle vibrational harmonisation from a Shungite pyramid and gentle care, a healing transformation can happen before your very eyes.

Oraphim had the pleasure of delivering Shungite workshops with Jane Osborne; her Shungite story is nothing short of extraordinary, following a near fatal skydiving accident, where her parachute failed to deploy, she was left paralysed from the neck down. However, thanks to her discovery of Shungite she requested that Shungite be placed at her feet and the mineraloid began to work its magic, reconnecting her nervous system and healing her bones. Jane gradually regained all her mobility, with the aid of many operations to tweak and improve her dexterity she is now fully able bodied without the need for any walking aids or support. Shungite was the driving force behind her incredible recovery when the doctors could do nothing, making it a truly miraculous story for Jane and the stone, where there's a will (fullerene) there's a way.

Using piezoelectric pressure and magnetic fields for serious bone fractures, the electrical flow can be restored as the bones themselves are also generating electrical current, this particular technique was developed by Dr Roth and published in Norman Doidge's book 'The Brain's Way of Healing'. worldwide, this technique has seen over 100,000 fractures healed, even when they were too fractured to heal by themselves, in Jane's case the Shungite was aiding the body to repair itself by remapping through these magnetic fields in a very powerful way.

Another influential resource is E L Rossi's engaging explanations and helpful exercises that cover many medical conditions and include case studies that defy medical explanations detailing healing and life changing events based on the patient's mind being in control. One patient's belief in a trial drug was so strong that the placebo effect, which is 33% effective, kicked into overdrive. Ultimately his own imagination worked as he wished to be well and this had worked his body into fixing itself. The chemical drug he believed was working was in the trial phase and turned out to be completely ineffective. When the scientific results were published, which contradicted his beliefs, the patient changed their beliefs and allowed the scientific reality to rule. They became rapidly unwell and passed away, when in fact it was recorded by the study that they had cured their condition but with no actual chemical medical help, this highlights just how powerful our mind is in both making us well and making us sick.

Cassie was given a divine response when she was asking her inner questions about the nature of the power we potentially hold within each of us, the reply was this 'If your inner voice held no power they wouldn't try to silence you.' How and what we think and feel is integral to our health.

Shungite has the ability to aid in the reprogramming of our beliefs, releasing old negative thought patterns and aiding the resonance with our original blueprint, but it's also about activation, unlocking new 'dormant' abilities beyond our imagination. What do we need to let go of now to create the space to let in something completely new?

What do we need to recognise in ourselves that is holding us back and what is getting ready to be released so that we can flourish and prevail in a way we have not even perceived yet?

Shungite is a wonder stone that can revitalise all kinds of dirty water, with the ability to remineralise and reprogramme our bodies with exquisite frequencies. This water is not only highly energised and healing, but it also has these effects on all who use it whether that is animal or human. With its quantum link to the mother lode at Karelia it appears to provide everything we need for us and our planet, what a wonderful place it is to be here now, in a wonderful body with a wonderful mind to match.

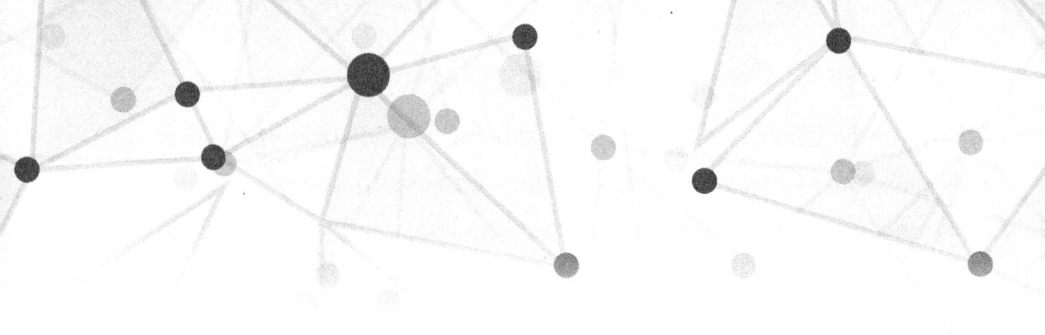

6

Quantum Remineralisation and Bio-Balancing

"The universe is energy. Vibrational energy. All energy vibrates. All matter is energy that has slowed down enough so that we can see it and touch it."
Nikola Tesla

Before the discovery of quantum physics Albert Einstein and his colleagues met in a private conference to discuss their frustrating inability to conduct experiments without directly influencing the outcomes through their observations which was altering their results. This new phenomenon was throwing into doubt the established scientific method defined by repeatable results being the standard scientific method, which led to the papers from this conference remaining unpublished for many years.

Quantum physicist Anton Zeilinger at the University of Vienna in Austria showed that quantum entanglement is possible for the fullerene C60 molecule; which challenged the previously held belief that only subatomic particles could behave as one over vast distances. This leads Cassie to delve into the weird world of Shungite testing and mineral exchange, deficiencies, vibrational coherence in the human biofield and the Shungite connection to activate our healing mineral blueprint of frequencies.

According to Inga Jurgelane and Janis Locs' research, "Shungite has good absorption properties towards various organic compounds and heavy metals, as well as exhibiting antibacterial properties." They also stated that Shungite affects the mineral content in the water when the stones are added for a period of a few weeks, with some minerals being much more elevated than others. In another study on the same topic minerals such as nickel, copper, lead, cadmium, zinc, chromium and arsenic were also similarly mentioned, performing in an elevated way but again only for the first two weeks of the study, so what is Shungite doing in those first two weeks of interaction with the water, or is it in fact interacting directly with the scientist's personal mineral deficiencies?

Oraphim were able to verify in an independent study that the lead level did not alter with the Shungite stones they provided for the test.

The Fullerene molecule that is found in Shungite is vibrating so fast that it contains the energetic signature of *everything* else; this is the key to recognising its action as a unique remineralising adaptogen. The material world equates to 0.01% of all things. The rest is energy. So although particles of matter seem dense, under a microscope they're as vast and well spread as the stars in the sky themselves.

One can hypothesise that researchers conducting experiments with Shungite are altering the outcomes of the experiment because Shungite simply interacts with those around it to affect them beneficially. This draws us to a new perspective: is it that the scientists themselves are altering the outcomes due to mineral depletion in their own bodies;

as the two weeks pass in Inga Jurgelane and Janis Locs' research the water had stopped having the particular mentioned minerals elevated, yet nothing about the stones is really any different, so much so that it defied their expectations too and they could not explain the sudden drop off either.

There is a need to look at this topic with a new perspective. The mystery around Shungite has not been explained in the mainstream yet so this confusion may cause people to have the wrong information about what is beneficial and what is actually harmful when it comes to using Shungite, if you are in any doubt about using the Shungite stones in your water then the Oraphim Toggles that attach to the outside of the taps and bottles are a great way to get the cleansing frequency and vibrational effects easily without touching the water. With the emergence of new technology it is potentially possible to gain greater insights into the intriguing nature and the way it interacts with mineral frequencies, because this mineral transformation is also known as 'remineralisation' and this is hailed as one of the great benefits of Shungite water.

It is interesting to learn that these particular minerals mentioned in both studies are required for the proper functioning of our bodies or for the purification and cleansing of the water to occur; we also need to separate the two mineral states: the harmful chemical version that people are concerned about and the natural safe version found in the mineral makeup of Shungite.

Both Russian researchers Ulyanova Irina Ilyinichna and Author Aurika Lukovkina talk about Shungite having the ability to selectively isolate mineral deficiencies in individuals and restoring the mineral balance through ion exchange. This in turn restores balance and health back to the body in a myriad of conditions; this is the valuable insight that we have been looking for and it answers why Shungite has elevated levels during the first weeks of everyone using it.

Shungite is able to perform an interactive cellular reading of our body's cells, actively scanning for the missing minerals in each cell, accessing Shungite mineral frequencies found at the Karelia mother lode to be coherently beneficial to the body and its processes and functions.

Not only does Shungite need further observation in new ways, but we need to examine the examiner, and the scientists need testing for mineral depletion before interacting with the Shungite sample. By conducting a study to measure mineral levels in different people who then prepare Shungite water from the same stones we would be able to further understand and verify what is really happening in a very exciting new way.

By using a number of testing methods such as live blood analysis, kinesiology (muscle testing), dowsing and bio resonance scanning with devices such as the Genius app, we would be able to identify each of the individuals' baseline mineral levels thus identifying any deficiencies. They would use the stones to test the mineral activity in the water and this could, for example, be performed a number of times over a month.

Bioresonance devices such as the 'Genius' used by Alison 'The Quantum Nurse' can isolate hundreds of individual elements in the body, reading their levels and changes. With Alison's 30 years of nursing experience she is able to see what the Genius picks up as depletions or elevations and the consequences of these as they are linked to our biological systems. Often bioresonance devices can detect when a person is wearing Shungite because the resonance of the Shungite is supporting the depleted systems and it means the readings are altered, showing just how Shungite is doing the exact job it needs to be doing to frequency balance the body, in most recent developments in 2024 Nancy L Hopkins and her team have added bioresonance frequencies for the silver infused S4 Shungite powder to the Genius app.

Some people simply use their own body as a pendulum, allowing the natural pull of the body towards the water when it has been transformed with Shungite as the indicator that their body wants to have this water. As we have explored the effects of the surfing hydrogen atoms earlier, the connection for the body and the glass of water to become one creates the natural pull towards each other, as they are in coherence with one another. Others can see their pets' reactions to Shungite water, with cats trying to paw for water from their owners' glasses or a dogs' new enthusiasm for Shungite 'tap' water instead of outdoor puddle water. Our personal approach is what matters, our own relationship to both water and our body is key, just add a little more inner love and appreciation along with your thank you to Shungite and water for perfect partnering.

So it really is a time for a whole new approach to science and education on many levels and learning what's really required for the proper functioning of our biological systems. We are experiencing a purposeful degradation of our water supply and with food poverty expanding the quality and what's available is diminishing rapidly. Shopping aisles staked with bags of sweet and salty chemicals and excitotoxins, fruit and veg coated in chemicals and far removed from its ancient ancestor. Truly beneficial foods being blacklisted and taxed beyond peoples budgets, the carbohydrate addicted nations are overeating to satiate the cravings from morning until night and it's a very difficult cycle to realise yet alone release from, but the reality of the situation is that the body actually requires very little sustenance when it is the right kind of *fats, proteins, water, light and minerals*.

7

Minerals On The Mind; How Does Shungite Do It?

The pharmaceutical industry is known for creating chemical compounds that may alleviate symptoms; this is a great business model for them, as the customer will keep using the products in the absence of knowledge that there may be safer natural alternatives or emotional or vibrational triggers that can be altered. Whilst the industry can supply additional pills to counter side effects, which is possibly by design; during Rich's 15 years working in operating theatres his views on the subject are that even our *thoughts* not just every thud or thump will have its deeper consequences on the physical in an energetic way, the removing of tissues and organs does not solve the issues the patient has, something created the problem in the first place. Whilst hospitals are excellent places to get broken bones fixed, the emotional input and output and the reactions of each of us must be dealt with or lived with, better that they be corrected before they manifest in our matter causing dis-ease he says.

What is an interesting question to ask is how many diseases and emotional responses are actually the side effects of parasites? The National Geographic stated that parasites have caused more deaths than all the wars in all known history. Again, have we been denied the knowledge of the old ways of using natural remedies for healthy living? As modern farming methods deplete the soil of its natural levels of Diatomaceous Earth, which is a natural antiparasitic we can plot the rising rates of IBS showing a correlation in parasite activity, Shungite is shown to be successful in the removal of 90% of Helminths' eggs from the gastrointestinal tract; what else can Shungite do for other parasitic infestations? Can Shungite remove the parasites in lupus sufferers, as lupus is also caused by a parasite? In a lady's first year of using Shungite she reduced her use of HCQ to one tablet a month now it's been two years and she has not needed any HCQ and the symptoms of lupus are gone; has Shungite successfully got rid of the lupus causing parasite?

By its very nature a natural compound or element cannot be patented or owned by any one person or company; so there's little to no financial incentive for pharmaceutical companies to produce natural beneficial products which have little to no harmful side effects when used appropriately. What can we make of the patents registered for the major agents being propagandised as natural mutated viruses, including C_vid 19 -US-patent 10130701.

Recently independent observations have been made regarding vital medicines and treatments which have been found to contain live parasites; there seems to be an invasion going on right under our noses and any and all methods of removing parasites is part of a daily healthy regime which is highly beneficial on many levels. The correct environment is crucial for parasites to thrive; their effects are wide ranging from loss of hearing and sight, diabetes, diseases and cancer. They love high sugar and carb diets and low frequencies even

Minerals On The Mind; How Does Shungite Do It? | 141

eating lots of vegetables which are carbs because they turn to sugar may require a second consideration. Is our planet and our bodies the perfect environments that they love, can parasites influence our thoughts and actions from dwelling deeply within us? *Yes they can.*

Changing ourselves and accessing new frequencies on both the biological and emotional level can make the parasite not want to stay inside us, as our cells react to changes and correct themselves through the use of Shungite the body will have greater access to the blueprint in our DNA which can be activated or deactivated by our emotions and thoughts.

Black Shungite's mineral makeup:

SiO^2	57.0	Silicon Dioxide is made up of silicon and oxygen
C	28.0	Carbon
TiO^2	0.2	Titanium dioxide exists in three phases: as rutile [1], anatase [1], and brookite [2]. These crystal phases assemble as octahedra, where six oxygen anions are shared by three titanium
Al^2O^2	4.3	Aluminium oxide (or aluminium (III) oxide) is a chemical compound of aluminium and oxygen
FeO	2.8	Iron oxide, also known as ferric oxide, is an inorganic compound with the chemical formula Fe2O3 that can be found in nature
MgO	1.2	Magnesium oxide (MgO). An inorganic compound that occurs in nature as the mineral Periclase. In aqueous media combines quickly with water to form magnesium hydroxide

CaO	0.3	Calcium Oxide. Drinking water is treated by using both hydrated and quicklime. It has a huge amount of usages for insecticides and medical purposes
Na_2O	0.2	Sodium oxide is a chemical compound with the formula Na2O. It is used in ceramics and glasses. It is a white solid but the compound is rarely encountered
K_2O	1.5	Potassium oxide (K_2O) is an ionic compound of potassium and oxygen. It is a base. This pale yellow solid is the simplest oxide of potassium
S	1.5	Sulphur is essential to life. It is a minor constituent of fats, body fluids, and skeletal minerals
H_2O chrys	3.0	Water is incorporated in chlorite, micas

Shungite Carbon 28%; Quartz 50%; composite silicates (micas, chlorite) – sulphides - 2

Hazardous factors: absent (none detected)

First Aid: product not poisonous to humans

No emergency incidents involving this product have ever been recorded

Handling and storing regulations: no special requirements

Personal safety rules and precautions: no special measures required

By effective rated activity of natural radiosondes Shungite is related to Grade 1

Shungite rock is not toxic

Ecologically safe

Shungite Healing Rooms Around the World

Patients with cardiac conditions were studied at the Voyenno Meditsinskiy Academy, many experienced undeniable advantage in achieving therapeutic improvements

White Springs Sanatorium Study Results:
Successfully alleviating symptoms from chronic illnesses of the respiratory and ear, nose and throat tract, also lessening musculoskeletal system swelling and pain alongside many other results attributed to Shungite since 2001

Long Lasting Benefits are Achievable:

Paint Your Own Protection & Create a Healing Space with Oraphim Silver Activated Shungite Powder

50gm Powder Per 2.5lt Paint

- Far-infrared ions released into the room for healing
- Quantum Emotional Body Healing
- Physical Healing & Wellbeing
- Thermal Insulating - Reducing Heating Bills
- Negative WiFi Attenuation & Blocking
- Surveillance Protection as used in Japan

Using a Shungite Room resulted in remarkable emotional trauma healing for the children of the Beslan theater massacre in September 2004

And Save Money on your Heating Bills!

Often we can get told a certain piece of information that turns out to be completely false yet we have based our choices on it in our lives. One great example of this is highlighted in the latest research by Francisco Gonzalez-Lima PhD, one of the world's leading neuroscientists, studying neurodegenerative conditions and the use of Methylene Blue; Alzheimer's which was widely linked to aluminium, which lead to many believing their pans to be the cause of Alzheimer's when this is not actually the cause. His groundbreaking research into a very cheap inexpensive dye called Methylene Blue offers hope to millions of potential Alzheimer's patients. However, this medical marvel is not a big profit maker for chemical companies, and this is the same for Shungite, it too is inexpensive and hailed as beneficial for neurodegenerative conditions. Dowsing results reported that it is highly beneficial to use Shungite around the head, with Oraphim producing unique fabric paint for their range of hats and eye masks, the effects can be felt tangibly as the Shungite energy infuses the head through the eyes, and you can even order some to use to paint your own clothing for EMF protection too.

Aluminium salts are artificially added as coagulants during water treatment to remove turbidity, organic matter and microorganisms; yet the removal of microorganisms and turbidity are listed benefits of using Shungite and indeed adding the Shungite does produce crystal clear water. Try using Shungite with a vase of cut flowers and see how much longer the water stays clear and the flowers please you with their blooms, even a flower's drooping stem will become firm and upright again too. It's fascinating that Shungite could be using the resonance of naturally occurring aluminium held within its makeup to do this vital job and does not add any harmful aluminium to water which would answer the question as to why the lakes around the Shungite in Karelia are pure enough to drink straight from the lake.

Magnesium oxide, present in Shungite (1.2%), is used for the relief of heartburn and indigestion, as an antacid, magnesium supplement and as a short term laxative. It's also used to improve symptoms of indigestion, all commonly cited beneficial effects of using Shungite water.

Calcium oxide found in Shungite is also used to treat drinking water by using both hydrated and quicklime. It has a huge amount of usages for insecticides and medical purposes, displaying a wide microbicidal action against harmful biofilms, fungi, heat resistant bacterial spores, bacteria and numerous viruses; again these are all the same actions that Shungite does too.

Sodium oxide is an ionic compound, containing a metal, sodium, a nonmetal and oxygen and the compounds that are oxidised are known to be conductive to electricity, these are vital electrolytes required for electric conductivity within the human body, Shungite's ability to balance these elements is perfect with the vital rewiring of the electrocircuits in both amputated and broken bones and we have indeed heard the miraculous story from Jane and her many broken bones healing.

Nickel labelled as a heavy metal is an essential micronutrient that is involved in lipid metabolism and increases hormonal activity. It makes its way through the human body via the respiratory tract, digestive system and skin. Nickel also plays a role in the cells of plants and some microorganisms due to its high electrical and thermal conductivity, which is important for electrical beings to have in the correct levels in the body. Finely divided nickel is employed to catalyse the hydrogenation of unsaturated organic compounds, such as fats and oils. The highest concentrations of nickel are found in the lungs, thyroid and adrenal glands (about 20-25 µg/kg wet weight). Most other organs (e.g. kidney, liver, brain) contain about

8-10 µg/kg wet weight; The World Health Organisation guidance covering the 'accepted' levels of nickel have changed over the years, and nickel even at its highest amount leaching into the water during the first two weeks of using new Shungite stones are still below the WHO's maximum; you would have to drink more than three litres per day and still not reach the WHO levels, but this is conveniently left out or not stated alongside studies stating elevated levels found in Shungite .

Metallic copper labelled as a heavy metal has many health benefits and is known to kill bacteria on contact including yeasts and viruses. With modern diets being overloaded with sugars and an emphasis on eating more fruit and veg which are essentially all carbs which turn into sugar, the bacterial load of most people needs extra help to clear, so it's definitely beneficial for us to have more copper; Shungite is stated as raising the levels in water samples fourfold, but with Shungite not being known to contain vast amounts of copper, it must simply be accessing the quantum copper mine via the quantumly entangled portal of the fullerene vacuum!

Historically arsenic and its compounds were used as a medicine in the treatment of such diseases as diabetes, psoriasis, syphilis, skin ulcers and joint diseases. Nowadays it is still used; especially in the treatment of patients with Acute Promyelocytic Leukaemia. Arsenic is also still contained in traditional Chinese medicine formulas and used for psoriasis, syphilis, asthma, joint pain (rheumatism), haemorrhoids, cough, itchiness and cancer to reduce swelling (as an anti-inflammatory agent), and as a general tonic and painkiller. Arsenic, a naturally occurring element, can combine with either inorganic or organic substances to form many different beneficial compounds. Inorganic arsenic compounds are in soils, sediments and groundwater. Organic arsenic compounds exist mainly in fish and shellfish. The health benefits of arsenic also match the reported health benefits of using Shungite, such as reducing inflammation, removing joint pain and increasing circulation in diabetes as well as a relief from itchy skin conditions such as psoriasis.

Shungite had a exceptional nullifying effect on the fluoride when tested by Cassie at Oraphim, with the results being visibly verifiable, as the red colour is kept dark by the lack of active fluoride, people are slowly coming to learn that artificially fluoridated products have a harmful aspect to them but there is still much to teach about the poisoning from this artificial compound.

Naturally occurring fluoride was discovered in Colorado as the locals had a brown staining to their teeth but no actual tooth decay in the local area to the springs. Upon further investigation the springs had higher levels of naturally occurring fluoride than other areas of the world. Nowadays, most people are artificially fluoride overdosed and calcium deficient and tooth decay is an epidemic in the US and UK. According to fluoridealert.org the '10 facts about fluoride' they state that the primary fluoride chemical (fluorosilicic acid) which is added to water is not considered a naturally occurring compound. Rather, it is a corrosive acid that is trapped by the air pollution control mechanisms of the phosphate fertiliser industry; the article delves deeper into this crucial issue explaining that fluoride gases are dangerous air pollutants that cause significant environmental damage, as a result the trapped fluoride acid is the most polluted chemical added to public water supplies and cosmetics.

We have been taught, trained / programmed to partake in daily rituals of chemical brushing of teeth with artificial fluoride causing a lot of health problems and it's not an easy one to solve overnight; how can we be sure that fluoride is so harmful in a different form from natures natural sources?

Ten years after Kingston started adding fluoride into the water supply (1945-55), health examiners found more cortical bone defects, anaemia and early puberty in school children who lived in fluoridated Newburgh NY as compared to non fluoridated Kingston NY. Fifty years later the children of Newburgh had more tooth decay and dental fluorosis than the children who were never fluoridated in Kingston NY.

Here are some additional facts to consider regarding fluoride in its toxic state:

- Studies have shown that fluorides can disrupt brain function
- Research conducted in China suggests that fluoride may lower intellectual abilities
- Fluoride has been identified as an endocrine disruptor
- Evidence indicates that fluoride exposure can affect thyroid function
- Certain forms of diabetes may become more severe due to excessive fluoride exposure

Allowing the body to restore its natural balance of healthy bacteria is crucial to preventing loose gums, shrinkage and tooth decay. By promoting the growth of good bacteria you can reap the benefits of a healthier mouth.

Shungite is a powerful antibacterial agent that literally kills bacteria on the teeth, this prevents the formation of plaque in the mouth just by brushing with a Shungite bristled toothbrush, additional benefits can be gained by removing the use of ingredients such as foaming agents sodium lauryl sulphate, which also disrupt the mouth's microbiome causing loose teeth and gums. Additionally, artificial water fluoridation, which is a form of enforced medication on mass populations, has negative side effects that can't be quantified and the cumulative effect of such fluoridation on multiple generations has caused untold damage. Thus natural sources of fluoride have a bad reputation and this is why it's important to learn a little more about these distinctive mineral state differences.

Ease Detoxification Headaches with Quantum Interaction

Do you experience headaches whilst detoxing? Try this simple method to alleviate the symptoms. Repeat the phrase 'Thank you, but that's too fast' silently in your mind. Within just three to five seconds you'll find that more often than not the detoxification headache symptoms will subside. Shungite just wants to make you the best you it can, quickly, but the body may want to detoxify more slowly as the symptoms and / or side effects of detoxing may feel uncomfortable.

8

Your Body the Vehicle for Your Soul

"Diseases of the mind have only two causes, they are totally opposite of each other. One way people become crazy is if their soul, or a part of their soul, has been lost. This usually happens because their soul has been stolen from them, but sometimes they may even decide unconsciously to give it away, perhaps in exchange for something they want. The second way people can become crazy is if they are overwhelmed and occupied by a foreign power" Excerpt spoken by Shaman Omai from 'Entering the Circle - Ancient Secrets of Siberian Wisdom' discovered by Russian Psychiatrist Olga Kharitidi.

What are we made up of? Why are we here?

Shaman Omai could be referring to parasites or elite controllers of society as both fit the description, the pushing of false beliefs and materialistic desires with a daily dose of taxation, tyranny and misery is experienced across the lands for the majority, what can we hope to achieve and experience? For some the selling of one's soul for fame and fortunes seems a fair trade, for others who are missing self-worth and have a desire to imitate the mainstream influences this desire is just powerful enough to be tricked out of keeping your soul intact in this lifetime. Negative experiences can cause weak energy fields that are unable to withstand the pressures of modern toxins and develop negative thoughts. The truth is slowly being revealed and experienced by many that our personal journey here is actually as a spirit in a body during the most satanic period in human history; it is said we will be known as 'the legends' for coming to Earth to witness the destruction of evil parasitic forces determined to keep the frequencies low and that we are here to aid in the raising of its humanities frequency and the liberation of the young souls trapped on our planet.

Spending time creating an inner place of peace, developing and cultivating this inner kingdom in communication with your Creator is key, for when you leave your body you are not destined to roam the world you see before you today, unable to interact and partake in the physical pleasures, which is all that disincarnate spirits want to do.

Cassie was due to work on a friends memorial commission, John had passed away convinced that there was nothing to expect or experience after his life, Cassie was guided to complete the pendant on a particular day; without any further hesitation she had carefully placed a lock of his hair into a green droplet setting with the Shungite, and as she prepared it for posting she found it strange that the instructions she was sensing was to send it without any additional notes, it felt odd to her to not include a 'hi' or 'best wishes,' to her friend but she quietly obeyed and sensed that in a way it was not from 'her' somehow. The next day she was contacted by her friend who asked "did you know it was my birthday today?" "No" Cassie replied; her friend explained that another acquaintance had sensed John's presence and given Andi a message the day before "John's here, he's going to come and visit you tomorrow." As Andi had returned from her errands the surprise packaged pendant containing John's lock of hair had arrived and was waiting for her on their doorstep. John had indeed come back to visit and had orchestrated the pendant's arrival for her birthday too; for a man with a belief of no afterlife he certainly was showing his presence to let his loved ones know his essence was experiencing a continuation which brought great joy to Andi.

Think of your body as a vehicle that connects your soul to the earthly experience. It is not who you are, but rather a vessel that helps you navigate through experiences in life. Rich explains it best: "If you could imagine a brochure for your holiday here on Earth, it would probably read something like this:

You will be provided with all that you need. Your amazing body suit plays an essential role in your journey.

- A fully automatic five sensory device, which takes a few years or so to get used to making it work, the device changes size and shape so you experience different views of the world as it grows

- Two models (male and female) with different functions which are equally great in different ways; they are made to be fully interactive with each other but take a bit of practice to getting the communicative settings to match at times

- Is able to complete many tasks at once and only requires minimal top ups of fuel and lubricant, don't worry though as the most beneficial lubricant falls from the sky (water) and collects in big networks all over the surface and the fuel is abundant growing and roaming about the place

- Fully compatible with the planet's environment: the waste products are fuel and food for the planet, as they are needed for a working biosphere. The carbon dioxide exhaled by the body suit is used to grow the fuel (trees and plants) for the device, similarly with the other two main excretions benefiting the plants to grow the planet when disposed of correctly - I mean just dig a small hole and pop the poop in it!

- If it gets scratched or broken it is able to activate a self repairing mode, the bioliving device generally has many early warning signs to let you know if you're using the wrong thought programmes

- Daily dance, stretch, smile, sleep, laugh, fart and fun settings

- Has occasional leaks from the eyes when extreme sorrow or extreme joy is experienced

- Wipe clean cover, fully submersible, even has fun in water

- The biggest organ is its skin cover, so be careful putting chemicals on the skin as they will transfer to the inside to harm the inner workings. Top Tip: Try Oraphim's' all natural organic Shungite body care range for magical effectiveness

- Sixth sense optimisation achieved with practise

- DNA next level upgrades available every 24,920 rotations of the sun or 323,960 full moons

- If you need any assistance whilst you're down here just send us a thought and look out for the answer

- When you're ready to leave, the body kit will sustainably recycle itself

- Price for this biodevice and package experience: Priceless

- Now go and enjoy your trip!

Your absolutely amazing body functions solely to aid your ability to actually 'feel' your way through each moment of the life experience.

Using Shungite to look after your vehicle is easily done with rapid repairing Shungite,

Antibacterial

Antiviral

Antihistamine

Anti-inflammatory

Antifungal

To name a few vital functions for aiding the body to rapidly repair, clean and refresh, ache and inflammation free Shungite is a fantastic resource.

The fascinating story of Olga Kharitidi's shamanistic experiences in the remote frozen Altai mountain villages of Siberia where she meets with a wise Shaman who offers deep insights and a profound understanding of our tasks here in this life, Umai outlines that individuals may feel lifeless if they only focus on the external world *"The next thing is the greatest secret I could tell you. We have the task of building two things whilst we are in our physical lives. Our first task is to construct the physical reality in which we live. The second task is the creation of ourselves - of that very self that lives within this outer reality."*

"Both tasks require equal attention. Keeping the balance between them is a very sacred and demanding art. As soon as we forget one task, the other can capture us and make us slaves forever." To heal and restore balance, you have the opportunity to consider using Shungite as a partner in this vital inner balancing work.

9

Shungite Body Care: A Magical Partnership

Oraphim and Susie Ashworth of Alchemisty have teamed up to create a powerful and effective range of body care, with a relief balm that can help with a wide range of skin conditions, muscle relief and inflammation. Arthritis being relieved within minutes much to the surprise and astonishment of sufferers. The key ingredient is Shungite which sends its healing frequencies to the exact problem area and enhances the carefully selected organic ingredients that work together in harmony to make this salve a miracle worker:

- Shungite has antiviral, antibacterial, antifungal and antihistamine properties
- Black seed oil nourishes and conditions the skin and is naturally anti-inflammatory, antifungal, antibacterial and antiseptic
- Safflower oil is rich in oleic acid which rejuvenates damaged skin and provides moisture to dry skin

- Calendula carrier oil is rich in salicylic acid which repairs skin and has calming and soothing properties

- Shea butter is an emollient with moisturising properties that soothes skin conditions

- Essential Lavender oil soothes and heals burns, relieves the itch and sting associated with bites and has antiseptic properties

- Frankincense oil aids in wound recovery and scar repair

- Cedarwood oil has antimicrobial and anti-inflammatory properties

- Thyme oil has antifungal and anti-inflammatory properties

This balm has become a household favourite with thousands of people using it to heal a variety of skin conditions, aches and pains, it's even effective in the farming environment with a single application curing a sheep's fungal foot rot. One single application also provided relief for a poor pug's itchy nose. The balm has healed Poison Ivy rash and provided a natural remedy for thrush; which has most ladies turning to the use of pharmaceutical antifungal treatments for.

Gail had an overnight result having used the balm on a patch of rosacea, and was pleased to report the next day that the patch had gone, with others leaving messages reporting similar results, and they are over the moon that they feel their skin is finally lovely and don't use makeup any more!

Back in 2018 before the balm was created, Cassie had tried adding the Shungite powder to many different things to make a remedy for a nasty patch of psoriasis on her shins, it was not possible to follow the body's messages to 'move' house to a new location at the time, unfortunately the Shungite turned the Aloe Vera gel to water, and water with Shungite dried and flaked off making a mess on the carpet, other ointment bases did not work to heal either, it was only once Susie had made the first batch that Cassie experienced the cooling, soothing relief, which was then followed by healing and there is no scarring left behind either.

"Works great on my daughter's eczema Thank you!"

"Thanks for everything! Great customer service and the items seem to be the highest quality."

"Thank you for the super-fast shipping, I received it much sooner than expected. This stuff is absolutely AMAZING! One of the only things that actually works for inflammation due to my lupus and eczema rashes. It aids in quick pain/itch relief, fast healing, and smells wonderful and absorbs so nicely. I love using this alone and also mixing it with other products for extra benefits. This shop has such awesome products and the customer service is outstanding! Thank you so much, Cassie!!!"

"Very speedy delivery. I am a return purchaser. I am buying this for a family member as they had used it recently for a burn on their hand. It stopped it blistering and helped it heal very quickly. Highly recommend. So handy to have in the house."

"Very speedy delivery. My partner tried it on his eczema which had flared up on his leg. He got his first full night's sleep after using it. No redness and no itching. Just a little goes a long way. Highly recommend. I am back to order another one" Milish 11 Apr, 2021

"Amazing! I really didn't know how much this was helping my skin until I ran out. Do yourself a favour and get a bigger size" Katie, Beauchamp 21 Apr, 2022

"Seems to have helped with a skin condition I have within a few days! A miracle indeed. I will definitely be buying more x" Ruth Lewis 04 Oct, 2021

"This balm has helped soothe a painful wrist and also a patch or two of eczema which I think is caused by EMF radiation. The skin is much less sore / itchy and nearly smooth now . Thank you." emmaycolford 18 Nov, 2022

"Earlier on this year I woke one morning with a nagging pain that was down the side of my hip and into the side of my stomach (not a tummy ache) more like a muscle twist or the old fashioned term a stitch in your side. After four days of this nagging pain I was really thinking I have to see the doctor as it wasn't going away. So in the bathroom that morning I thought hang on a minute I had a small amount of the Rescue Balm left over so I thought oh well I'll rub it on where the pain was. Washed my face, did my teeth and suddenly realised that pain was gone completely, I know it seems impossible but honestly that is genuinely what happened, and what's more that pain has never returned.

Can I fully explain this….no other than this was the Shungite Balm. So there you go that was my experience AMAZING." Denise (Buxton)

"Great high quality product. Works really well for joint pain. Shipped fast and very nice seller."

"This is the best on bug bites! The sting/itch instantly goes away!"

"Nice product. Goes on smooth with a nice fragrance. It's definitely doing something! Thanks," Brie

"This product is absolutely amazing. I've been juggling with atopic dermatitis following an ongoing itch…inflammation gone, itching gone…haven't had to use Benadryl in almost a week. Thank you"

"Love it! Works as a lip balm, scar treatment, to heal chapped lips, on/inside the nostrils, keeps insect bites from itching and of course as an overall balm for dry/sensitive/itchy skin and a huge thank you for the beautiful gift! Love it"

"Really great! It made my scars fade much more and keeps the healing itchiness away. Already ordered backup"

"Very happy with this item. It smells amazing and my it's so nice on my skin. When getting items like this you always want to test how effective they are in helping you. I was bitten by a mosquito in London on my hand, super itchy as we all know, I applied the cream, and after 3 minutes I totally forgot I was ever bitten. I just got back from Paris and was bitten twice there too, the cream I'm sure has many many amazing uses, but I can confirm for me, and these mosquito bites it works perfectly. It's a must to keep with you. Would recommend and order again!"

"Have nasty looking mosquito bite scars on my arms. I bought the rescued balm from you and have been using it since. I must tell you that on the 5th (!) day of using it, my scars were reduced by I would say 70%. Nothing that I used in the past worked. So I'm grateful to you for sharing your products with me. I know you wouldn't expect anything else from Shungite, for me it's something new and it started working sooo quickly".

"I use the bottle toggle and the bracelet too; I'm constantly in high spirits and have lots of energy." Eva Mazurek

Are you tired of dealing with blemishes and other skin issues? It's time to try out the Shungite Soap and Rescued Balm combination because Shungite has the scientific reasoning behind its miracle skin rejuvenation.

Research published by the NIH shows that fullerenes which are found in Shungite can significantly reduce the average number of inflammatory lesions, with a reduction rate of 23.2% and 37.8% respectively and the numbers of pustules also significantly decreased by an amazing 87.6%. Further testing revealed that fullerenes can inhibit sebum production which is the primary cause of acne. After eight weeks of treatment with Shungite the water content of the skin increased significantly ($P < 0.05$), making Oraphim's Shungite Soap perfect for balancing oily or dry skin; and the combination of Shungite water, soap and balm is the rapid skin rejuvenating miracle people with problem skin love - restoring their skin to a radiant beautiful glow.

Here are some testimonials:

"This is awesome soap. It smells wonderful, and seriously clears and cleans on all levels. Many thanks"

"Really fast delivery of all my items very impressed! The balm and soap are AMAZING! Soap is very silky soft, a pleasant, gentle fragrance and have to say, my skin looks and feels great. Balm is ultra soothing for dry, red skin patches. Will definitely be back for a lot more.

I first had this as a free sample with a different purchase and it was amazing I had to order more! I have a lot of freckles and irritated skin but after 3 days of use my freckles have minimised and my skin feels great. Thank you x"

"Thank you. Very nice soap with a beautiful fragrance. The skin is soft and delicious after washing with this soap"

"I showered with the Shungite soap for the first time, using it as a shampoo bar as well. It felt very relaxing and my hair has never felt so soft!" S. Rowley

The Benefits of Using Shungite Deodorant

Knowing that Shungite has antibacterial properties led to the creation of a very special Shungite deodorant which has produced amazing results. Not only is it 100% chemical free and organic but it also eliminates body odour caused by bacteria in the armpit leaving behind a divine scent. You can confidently go about your day without worrying about any unpleasant smells after physical activity. Additionally the deodorant doubles as a perfume bar so try applying a dab to your pulse points for an all-day fragrance.

The Deodorant also contains castor oil which aids in the dissolving and breaking up of internal growths and cancers, so it's a great product for not causing these issues in the first place and could well help with healing the body from the use of chemical saturated products which may have been used previously.

"Love love this deodorant. Smells amazing and I feel so clean after I use it. Will not use any other deodorant. Will absolutely keep ordering. Received within a week. Thank you for this wonderful product". Nancy A 21 Jun, 2021

"I will forever be using this thank you" Nethers 20 Jun, 2021

"Exceeded expectations, really uplifting fragrance and reliable too" Kat 04 Oct, 2021

"This is roll on deodorant which I have never been a big fan of but this stuff I am going to keep using. It smells brilliant and works great for deodorant and antiperspirant. Then of course it contains Shungite" John 10 Jul, 2021

"Smells divine – and now so do I." Catherine 04 Jun, 2021

Experience the Healing Powers of Shungite with Oraphim's Minty Lip Balm!

Who wouldn't want special Shungite miracle kisses with Oraphim's marvellous minty lip balm? It's that simple - rapid repair and protection all winter long, all natural with 100% organic ingredients and silver infused Shungite with no petrochemicals, or nasty unnatural ingredients.

It's worth noting that despite the bad press oil gets for being accused of being a 'fossil fuel' when technically it's not one, there is still a big agenda to reduce its use in our day to day lives, most commercially available medicines and body care products are made from petroleum. Petroleum jelly for example is the base for most lip balms, once people realise that they are actually ingesting petroleum derived products they want to find a safe and effective alternative which Oraphim provides. But don't just take our word for it, check out these glowing product reviews!

"My everyday lip balm now! Super speedy delivery and packaged with love" Tina 19 Oct, 2021 5 out of 5 stars

"Excellent as always" Philipp V. *18 Sep, 2021 5 out of 5 stars*

"The lip balm feels great and lovely and fresh. Will last ages too." Katy *15 Apr, 2021 5 out of 5 stars*

"Absolutely love this lip balm it's very soothing when it goes on and not overpowering mint I also love the tin it's in"

Super Mineral Detoxing - Sensory Soak with Shungite too

Detoxing in heavenly scents, ion exchange and magnesium rebalancing are all vital for the healthy body, Oraphim's Shungite

Bath Salts have proven themselves time and time again to work miracles for people with chronic pain; even putting their hands or feet in a bowl with the salts they experienced reduction in pain levels, as Michelle experienced suffering with a damaged knee, and Sue with her back after a few minutes of soaking both had reduced pain relief.

"These salts smell absolutely incredible! ... Seller was so kind and sent some extra little freebie samples which made my day" 5 out of 5 stars Tabitha 21 Dec, 2021

*"These bath salts are lovely and smell wonderful. Thank you for the free gifts as well. The poppy seed soap has the best smell. Delivery was very fast, fully recommended buying from this seller." * 5 out of 5 stars Michele Beckenham 19 Sep, 2021

"This is probably the best bath salt I have used albeit quite expensive for the amount you get. It deserves to be worth more than most though because of the amazing ingredients and even a variety of different types of salt. You get epsom, pink Himalayan, AND Dead Sea salts in here which I have never seen before. It smells amazing and is sensational on the skin. 10/10" 5 out of 5 stars John 10 Jul, 2021

"These are one of the best bath salts I've tried; every wonderful thing is in it. Smells really good too!" 5 out of 5 stars Mia 15 Nov, 2021.

A little Shungite love goes a very long way!

The Versatility of Shungite body butter is loved by both genders, and offers more than just moisturising, as Dorit explains that she has flexibility back from just using her first tub.

Shungite is a versatile mineral that can be incredibly beneficial for both physical and emotional wellbeing. That is why our body butter containing Shungite is loved by all who try it.

"Even just opening the jar of this body butter sends me straight to heaven! The smell, the texture, the ingredients! Oh my! It applies so smoothly; even on my face it doesn't feel heavy, and I forget that I have it on, yet my skin looks and feels amazing! Thank you for creating this magic" 5 out of 5 stars   Adelaida 28 May, 2021

"I have bought from Oraphim several times now and their products are superb. Highly recommend the soap and body butter, it is absolutely amazing! Service and delivery exceptional. Thank you for such stunning products. I look forward to purchasing again soon." Nicola 03 Aug, 2021

"Lovely product smells wonderful and great for dry skin I highly recommend will definitely be purchasing again .. Thank Oraphim" 5 out of 5 stars Susie 23 Jun, 2021

"I love these products, all of them… at 46 years of age I have noticed over the past couple years a few restrictions with the movement of my body, last night I was able to touch fingers when I reached a hand behind down my back and the other up behind my back… I have movement again. Yippeeeeee this is my 2nd tub, ready for when my first runs out" 5 out of 5 stars   Listing review by Dorit Phipps

10

Shungite Eye Masks and Their Benefits

Shungite eye masks have become an Oraphim best selling item, they have a wide range of benefits and numerous reports of successful outcomes, these include improved sleep patterns, vivid dreams, migraine relief and even rapid eye repair. In fact testimonials from users have claimed that they no longer need to wear glasses as often after using the eye masks for a short while.

Inspired during her days working as a care assistant Cassie wanted to help her client who underwent terrifying eye injections delivered directly into each eyeball with no anaesthetic for their macular degenerative condition. The treatment plan for these injections was scheduled for every four months or so. Shortly after the first time Lizzie wore her eye mask, which relieved the ache from the injections helping reduce the trauma too, the ophthalmologist remarked that her eyesight had improved. Well that was the first time that had been recorded as an improvement in the four years Cassie had known her client, but surely it was just a coincidence?

"I LOVE this sleeping mask! First, it got rid of my eye pain and headache. I have been sleeping better since getting/wearing this mask. My sleep is deeper and more restful. I have other sleep masks and I don't feel as rested in the morning with them as I do with this mask. Positioned correctly it blocks the light beautifully. The gift of the disks for inside the shoe were great. I love walking with Shungite in my shoes. Highly recommend!" noell2730

"I recommend this Seller and the product, definitely. The Shungite face mask gives my eyes instant relief after I have been on the computer or my phone for a while!! Less headaches and eye strain, I really believe this is helping. The product was shipped quickly and I am very pleased. Thanks so much!" Robyn Patrick-Mayer

"Mask is perfect, glad it has the extra bit attached to fit around my melon head. I find I have a better sleep with my mask and my eyes do feel that bit better too. **I've stopped wearing my glasses as often too.** *This is one of my favourite shops"* Dorit

Maybe it wasn't a coincidence after all, thanks to Dorit's testimonial. Shungite is truly transformational, it is a powerful cleanser for water and our eyes are 98% water, so the healing effects are remarkable.

All you have to decide on is how you want to incorporate Shungite into your daily life and there will be a form of Shungite that will work with you; is there something that you want to make better? Making your own Shungite application is often not as difficult as you might expect, you can always take inspiration from the products Cassie, Rich and Susie have to offer. Whether it's painting your own fabric or applying the silver activated powder to your decorating or donating the powder to your local beekeeper, whatever you decide to do, it's a decision the whole world could benefit from as you find your joy.

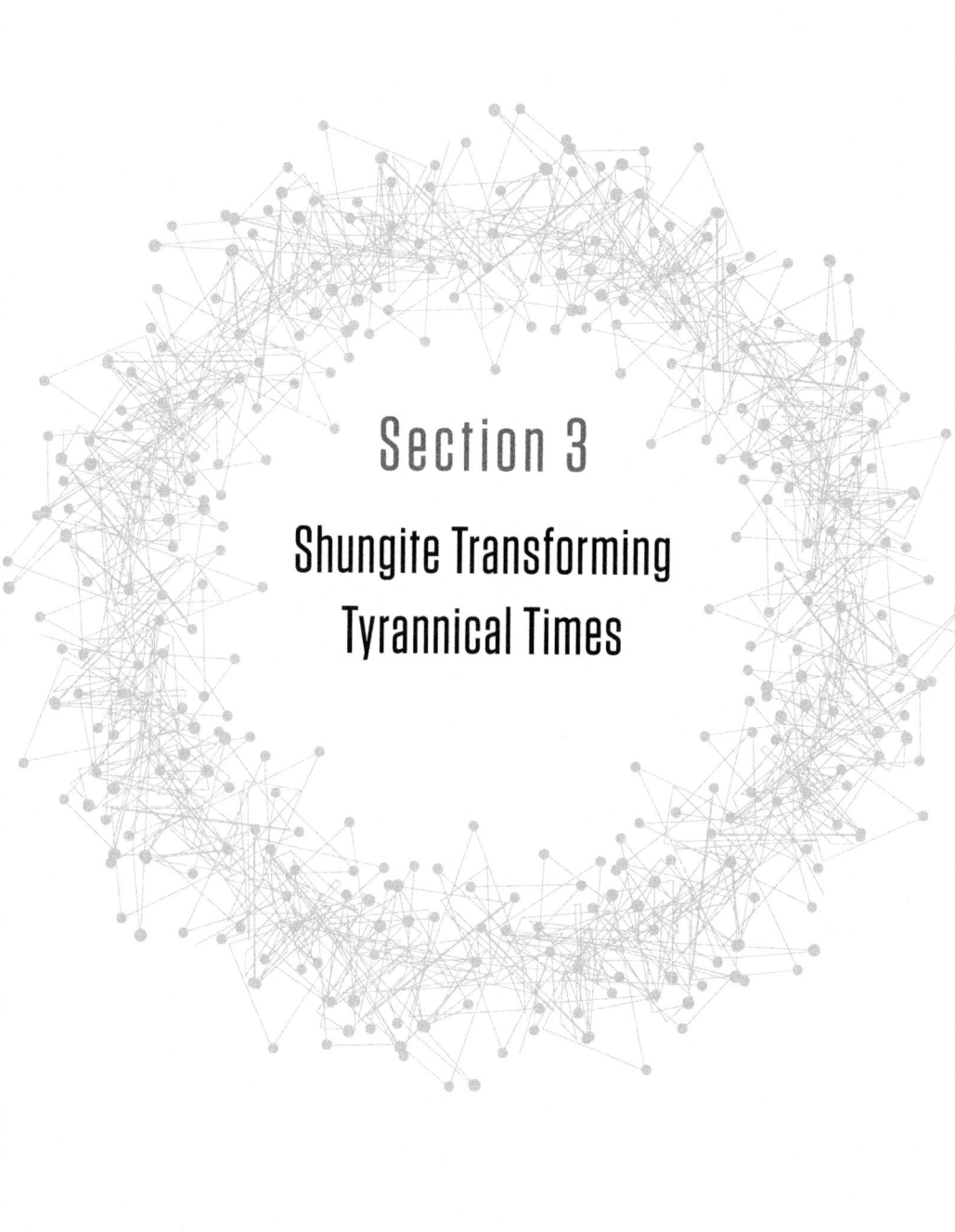

Section 3

Shungite Transforming Tyrannical Times

1

The Battle for Your Attention, Time, Hearts and Minds

"Concerning the manner of work in civilised States, these States are composed of three classes - a class which does not even pretend to work, a class which pretends to work but which produces nothing and a class which works, but is compelled by the other two classes to do work which is often unproductive"
William Morris 1834-96 (Useful Work v. Useless Toil)

For most people there are simply not enough hours in the day to do much more than provide for their basic needs, and it's been cleverly designed that way. The rich and powerful have controlled and exploited the patchwork of interconnected religions, society and cultures to steal our time and subdue our spirits to say the least. The conflicting histories we are taught play on our emotions leaving us conquered and divided. It's crucial to grasp the extent of the manipulation, coercion and control exerted over humanity for thousands of years, culminating in the current engineered crisis. By exploring the next chapters, which cover various cultures and histories going back nearly 4000 years with Shungites' pivotal role in specific circumstances including the most recent appearance of a glowing ball exploding over the Karelian deposit that has changed our world forever; we will gain a deeper understanding and appreciation of our divine gifts and place in the current times with a new wonder for ourselves as we establish our reconnection to each other; has our own DNA got something special to show to us?

Cassie and Rich had carved out a meagre existence living in their motor home with others at an 'off grid community' encampment, without running water and creature comforts for nearly ten years to be able to devote time to learning and searching for working solutions to modern slavery and governmental overreach. Whilst supporting themselves working in the arts and care sectors. Off grid living is a challenging lifestyle which has become a dream for many wanting to escape the 'rat race'; living this way strips away the façade and exposes one's true nature and that of the government's control agenda and their need for our assimilation into their system. For those of us on the lower rungs of society who have a wish to disengage from the 'system', inspired by the powerful insights of Robert Buckminster Fuller *"to create a new reality"*, must have eyes to see the faults in the current one with enough courage to gently collect the skills and tools to exist in two very different paradigms, one being the dystopia system with the ability to see the hypocrisy of the ruling class and with an ability to also see what they may be diverting the tax money to and the other a beautiful utopia of beneficial cooperations existing as divine souls. In essence the current reality of our common situation, regardless of one's material possessions or perceived security, is that we are all peasants and paupers, not to belittle anyone, but to acknowledge our commonality, the 'P' on all of our passports signifies our status as 'paupers' together.

Cassie's son once told her that he was more intelligent than she was, to which she replied "thank God for that, otherwise we are all stuffed." This honest interaction highlights the essence of personal growth and the proper place for competitiveness which is not between the generations which can often be seen in large parts of impoverished society; surely life should be getting easier as each generation gains technological advances that surpass the previous generation. Yet we need to be smarter and avoid being overly reliant on smart devices. We should naturally wish our children to surpass us for the betterment of humanity, and by developing balanced individuals who find solace in moments of solitude to connect with nature and their Creator for fulfilment, instead of relying on fast food and technology, removed from spirituality which only leaves many craving more materialistic accoutrements and hedonistic pastimes can we break the entropic cycles?

Our personal and family histories, communities and relationships are becoming further lost to technological advances requiring even deeper integration into the 'system' and an over reliance on a 'nanny state' when *can* we grow up and take full responsibility when the overbearing state makes ever increasing demands. This is increasingly difficult when we are, for large parts of society, squeezed and pressured to breaking point and parents even begrudge the surpassing of their own intellect by their children due to their own personal traumas and day to day hardships, it seems as though even the joy is squeezed from our spirits.

Cassie offers a unique perspective on personal development, through exploring hidden religions and bridging the gap between pagan rites, Christian history and the mathematical summing up of our DNA you may find we have more in common to unite us all than might have been considered before. Those who seek to control us by their gaslighting and dividing tactics don't want us to *imagine* standing together against them. Throughout history people have organised and built communities, only to have them infiltrated and subverted by those in power and modern times are no different. Christians and pagans have both been targeted, experiencing persecution and large scale massacres for centuries, we may have lost the religious context to our daily lives in modern times but we have not lost the battle.

By examining these two sects that were both forced to hide their beliefs we will learn who disguised their teachings in the Tarot, we can then uncover lost spiritual knowledge that holds the key to inner fulfilment and as we revisit the past we will see the present world events in a new and revealing way, which will provide the answers to why Shungite is now a very difficult commodity to import out of Russia and into your life.

What is the significance of understanding our true cultural heritage in today's society? Whilst Shungite's medicinal and scientific properties are gaining popularity, Shungite is often categorised with alternative healing practices, often found in crystal, New Age Shops and at Mind Body Spirit Fairs alongside alternatives such as crystal therapy, witchcraft and paganism; which means it can be overlooked, misunderstood and misrepresented, when it has major scientific reasoning as to why it is truly effective and useful to all of us.

Many people are drawn to the New Age Movement and more are now turning to mediums, and with modern 'manifestation' and quantum manipulation techniques they may find inspiration and direction they are seeking and class this as 'spirituality' however it is often delivered through a third party paid intermediary. This often stems from pantheism and a reverence for lesser gods and their expressions in our world with the avoidance or exclusion of connecting to a greater Creator, some are even being guided by trickster disincarnate spirits, say hello to roaming spirit DIV_C-91! = C_vid-19.

Could it be that the pagan interpretation of the messages delivered from the internal conversation in the void through ritual and ceremony actually be the answers from the Creator, as the answers that come from the Creator can be expressed all around us in our environment which led to the rise of pantheism and elemental worship. Zarathustra founded the first monotheistic religion in the world, challenging the existing traditions of the ancient Iranian religion around 1800 BC. His teachings focused on developing good and kind ways of being in peace with all living beings, and this had an impact on Plato, Pythagoras, Judaism, Christianity and Islam, his watery epiphany gave him insights that there was a solo divine creator to his experience.

This next excerpt from 'Entering the Circle' - Ancient Secrets of Siberian Wisdom discovered by Russian Psychiatrist Olga Kharitidi puts a beautiful and succinct view of this connection to our inner beings observer guides: *"Every human has a particular entity that inhibits the place of their Spirit Lake. These entities exist within this inner space, waiting at the entrance of Belovodia. I call this entity the Spirit Twin, but its name could also be Spirit Helper, Shadow Watcher, Spirit Guide or Inner Guardian."* When we are created and kept as nature prescribed this is the connection we are born with and can instantly connect too, due to the separation and diluting of cultures many are very often unaware of this reality and attention is filled with modern distractions.

When our lives have been fully illuminated by the pure light of our inner observer, everything we do becomes much easier, this is a common experience of working with Shungite which strengthens your energy field and allows you to have a greater connection to your inner guidance; When we consider the possible implications of many having been severed from their connection to the 'Spirit Twin', 'Higher Self' or as many others call it 'God' by the 'krisper' gene editing DIV_C-91 injections we can see that this time in history is unlike any other and that the clues were there all along, a nefarious plan entitled the name of a very negative spirit indeed.

It's never too late to begin to make a spirit reconnection, to enhance and strengthen your frequency with loving energy with Shungite to facilitate the process of keeping safe your soul and detoxifying.

The Spirit Twins: "*To begin with they are intimately connected with the ultimate purpose given to each person at birth. They are also pure observers set apart and invulnerable to the influences of the outer world. They are the holders of the primal essences of our natal beings. If called upon in the proper way and circumstances, they can be important helpers to us in performing actions that move us in the direction of our correct purpose*"

The truth of the matter is that we are ultimately caring beings, with only the deepest desires to help others as others help us, not to harm them, which is why for most they simply can not conceive of the atrocities of the current situation, being naive and gullible are beautiful human qualities that are easily taken advantage of by corrupted individuals, and we have been tricked into behaving against our innate sensibilities on a daily basis as simply the government demands us to apply and purchase 'lie-sences' for the many activities that are simply modern essentials.

Our goal next is to uncover why certain groups in history were targeted and fragmented, their knowledge and insights which were classified as 'unacceptable antiestablishment' beliefs by the Roman rulers of the time, so they cleverly concealed spiritual teachings into the divination Tarot cards of today; it is believed that this obscured spiritual knowledge holds the key to achieving true fulfilment and that these divination cards are the hidden 'Challis' and also at the same time the 'Holy Grail' which were later picked up by the gypsies for fortune reading as they entered Northern France.

Humanity has the capacity for greatness, and what is true is that individuals always strive to do their best. However, when tyrannical rules are imposed upon us, our behaviour and actions can be coerced to fulfil the agendas of those in power just to survive; as is prevalent in communist cultures. We do not actually need the state or the church to dictate what is right and wrong, but instead acting out of our innate good conscience and treating others as we would like to be treated is simple to instil and implement. By developing an inner path to a higher connection with the Creator, through help from our Spirit Twin or Higher Self, we can find greater guidance, joy and protection, it's only the need for manipulated money systems to survive that twists our actions to harm others and to keep us away from really getting to know who we are and what we are.

"The next step will be one you are already taking, which is to realise that there is another self that creates one's personal reality. Your Heart Self, your genuine self, is the one responsible for this creation; each person must experience it to understand." Excerpt from 'Entering the Circle - Ancient Secrets of Siberian wisdom discovered by Russian Psychiatrist Olga Kharitidi

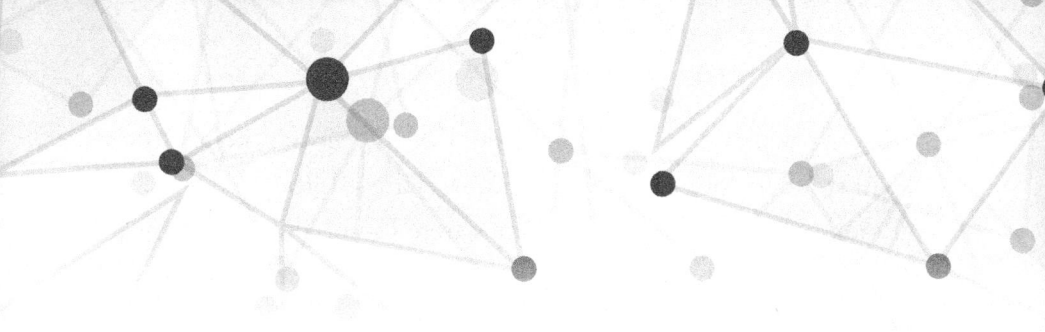

2

Survival of the Soul and the Shungite Detox

"For the evolution of the species, only the fittest survive." Dr Peter Gladden explains that modern diseases are not inherited illnesses but purposeful poisonings.

The World was changed forever when a prophesied event preceding the government 'stay at home' orders were announced when over the Shungite deposit in Karelia a blue glowing ball appeared and exploded in mid air, captured on CCTV,10 days before lockdowns were implemented. Many people have reported that Shungite has helped them avoid the symptoms of C_vid. But what really is C_vid 19, can it be pinpointed to being one thing such as a virus; or is it a multipronged attack of some sort?

There is still much to come to light regarding the reporting of deaths that were falsely attributed to create a 'pandemic' which then inspired many people into taking an experimental medicine; on the 24th September 2023 four New Zealand Government Officials: Christopher John Hipkins, Andrew James Little, Ashley Robin Bloomfield and Christopher James were found guilty for their part in actions that breached the 'He Wataputanga' declaration that led to serious C_vid 19 crimes against the sovereign peoples of New Zealand.

During a discussion hosted by John Lockland, Director of 'Foreign for Domestic International,' at the European Parliament in October 2023 evidence was presented that the C_VID-19 vaccine contained different ingredients than those that were officially approved, leading to numerous injuries since its implementation. According to a comprehensive guide published by the State of the Nation (SOTN) in August 2021 'Shungite C60 plays a crucial role in finding a lifesaving remedy;' with further evidence that undeclared and potentially toxic ingredients are being added to the experimental mRNA treatments, reported Dr Ardis and also by Professor Floyd who has over 30 years of study dedicated to an enzyme related to rattlesnake venom.

Repairing the damage is potentially clinically possible as it was reported that the fullerene C60 (black Shungite) nanoparticles were effective in treating heart inflammation in rats and that it is a promising and potentially effective therapy for the treatment of heart diseases associated with inflammation in humans; this was the conclusion of the PubMed study 23rd February 2023 carried out by Seda Beyaz and team; when we consider that myocarditis is inflammation of the heart and is a known and reported side effect for the C_vid treatment affecting large numbers of young people, who have now been administered this experimental 'treatment' we need to be administering a remedy on a mass scale now too.

Fullerenes found in Shungite are the perfect size to fit into the DNA and RNA of the human body, when looking for solutions to what could possibly repair DNA, RNA and inflammation, including those caused by the 'Krisper mRN_ gene editing' and its significance in DNA rewriting we do have a possible solution in fullerenes and Shungite.

Former Pfizer VP, Dr Mike Yead_n states *"Do not take anything with the word VACCINE on it, especially mR_A or emergency."* Why would he say that so categorically?

For the full coverage of the pandemic from the perspective of an uncensored comprehensive academic review the NIH article lays out in its entirety certain scientific and media suppression that has taken place on many levels. Blaylock RL. C_VID UPDATE: What is the truth? Surg Neurol Int 2022;13:167 https://www.ncbi.nlm.nih.gov/pmc/articles/PMC9062939/

The State of the Nation (SOTN) stated that supercharged C60 found in Shungite is a powerful antioxidant that may be the most potent yet known, with its sphere-like structure forming the only molecule of a single element. Whilst statistics show a 99.9% recovery rate from C_VID-19, it's staggering to note that the 'mortality rate' has actually tripled since the mRN_ 'cure' was introduced. It's possible that logical people can see that the 'cure' maybe responsible for the damage being caused to the populace, and there are now many more people researching possible lifesaving solutions, the article concluded by stating that Shungite "may be the most powerful antioxidant yet known, performing the antioxidant action of Superoxide Dismutase, Glutathione, Catalase and CoQ10"

'Fullerenes have anti-inflammatory, antiviral, antioxidant and anti HIV properties' reported the NIH on the 27th July 2021.

Professor Andrievsky stated that Shungite is "30 times more effective than activated charcoal in removing free radicals and antioxidants safely from the body". Although each detoxification agent has its own benefits, Shungite stands out because it combines them all into a simple solution. It's no wonder that Shungite receives such high regard for its effectiveness.

To take each of those detoxification elements separately Superoxide dismutase (SOD) is an enzyme which is present in all living cells which catalyses chemical reactions in the body. By breaking down harmful oxygen molecules, SOD helps to prevent damage to tissues.

Shungite mimics the actions of Glutathione which has been discovered to be a potent antioxidant that can do wonders for antiaging, preventing cancers and even helps treat autism. In addition to these primary benefits here is a comprehensive list of other advantages:

- Antioxidant
- Regenerates cells
- Boosts sperm count
- Detoxifies and heals liver
- Detoxifies heavy metals
- Supports immune function
- Rescues oxidative stress
- Helps heal psoriasis and other skin conditions
- Helps treat autoimmune diseases
- Reduces diabetes
- Treats respiratory disease
- Improves sleep
- Increases energy
- Relieves muscle and joint discomfort
- Improves athletic performance

Catalase is a key enzyme which uses hydrogen peroxide, a nonradical ROS, as its substrate. This enzyme is responsible for neutralisation through decomposition of hydrogen peroxide, thereby maintaining an optimum level of the molecule in the cell which is also essential for cellular signalling processes.

CoQ10 is a significant substance that facilitates the conversion of food into energy. It is present in almost every cell in the body and serves as a potent antioxidant. Free radicals are harmful particles in the body that can damage cell membranes, tamper with DNA, and even cause cell death. Luckily CoQ10 helps fight these destructive radicals and Shungite is able to mimic this and even make your food flavours enhanced as Cassie's care client exclaimed one day that her Marmite tasted *Marmitier!*

With Shungite detoxifying and its potential for repairing damage from 'Krisper' gene editing we may see many more recovery stories than before. Moreover the dormant DNA in our cells may hold untapped potential, leading to abilities beyond our imagination but could having lowered frequencies from oppression and tyrannical overlords be stifling our creative expressions and thoughts?

Why now; what is it about this particular time in history that has made your soul want to come here?

The Schumann Resonances are a set of frequencies produced by electromagnetic waves in the Earth's lower ionosphere, unusually set at a continuous range of 7.83 Hz to a maximum of 33.8 Hz, this vibration is called the Earth's 'heartbeat', and now gaining a greater audience. These frequencies are being witnessed by millions of excited souls all over the planet as they are changing often and showing readings that are unlike any previous readings ever recorded; it's as if the Earth's heartbeat is getting quicker, coinciding with the Earth being excited by the photon cloud we are now passing through. Another coincidence is the fact that our sun has entered a solar cycle 25 and is now delivering plasma energy to Earth in mass coronal ejections unlike the quiet period of inactivity that was seen before, and finally that the magnetic shielding which would normally provide perfectly adequate protection to all these external threats happens to be at its all time lowest protection level. The culmination of all of these factors is that there are many new galactic frequencies bathing us and our earth in a concoction of exquisite new cosmic vibrations. That outlines the major extraordinary occurrences arriving all at once for these times we are living in, where the most common name happens to be *Noah*, so we are in the times of *Noah!* (for more information on cosmic frequencies and the sun's activity check out **Ben Davidson** at https://spaceweathernews.com)

This unprecedented combination of factors are playing a huge part in the changes occurring here now and in the very near future; What can we do to stay tuned to the new frequencies and align with new possibilities, take a moment now just to imagine your ideal reality and generate a little heart flutter of anticipation at the same time…. In Joy.

Does our mass awakening and loving hearts have disastrous consequences for the ruling Elite?

Is what you *know* and how you *feel* about it really that important to the balance of power?

These and many more questions are inherent to our comprehending of just how integral we are to the outcome of the current Earth's transition; to awakening to the keys to the inner kingdom and the imminent event that's due to transform *us* and our *planet, expect the unexpected, or are there clues and signs we can look to for guidance?*

3

The Blue Star Kachina: A World Changing Event

When we think about the most significant event that occurred in early 2020 the first thing that comes to most people's mind is the global lock-downs. However, this wasn't the only or most critical event that took place that fateful February. You are about to discover what truly transformed our world and you might even be holding a piece of it as you read this book; a rare element that is finding its way into the hearts of many.

On the eve of our upheaval we received unexpected help from a little known source to most: Shungite, a mineraloid which you have now explored to great lengths for its healing and transformational properties, was on its way for the biggest transformation in history as out of nowhere it increased its frequency. On the 21st February 2020 a blue glowing ball descended from space and exploded over the mother lode of Shungite in Karelia. Since then all Shungite on the planet raised its frequencies to greater than 5G. Walt Silva had previous readings of 256 GHz, the blue 'meteorite / star' arrived so he took his measurements again and the frequency measured 1298 GHz, in late 2023 the frequency had climbed again, and his latest measurements are recorded at 70,000 GHz.

What is fascinating is that these new higher frequencies now exceed the telecommunications 5G frequencies, and according to the law of resonance, higher frequencies transform lower frequencies. This event also aligns with the Hopi Prophecy of the Blue Star Kachina, which states that the arrival of the Blue Star Kachina or Saquasohuh signifies the start of a new world.

In Frank Waters' writings, the Blue Star Kachina is a spirit that appears in the form of a blue star and is said to be the ninth and final sign before the 'Day of Purification', a cataclysmic event that will lead to the destruction of the World; when Nancy L Hopkins explored this event through remote viewing she requested to be taken to the source of the blue object, she was immediately taken far out to space and encountered a being with an immense calm but the wish to see his face was denied.

It is evident that something is coming to an end, and the controllers are clinging onto their power desperately, as all they have is more rules, restrictions, surveillance, control and tyranny. Have we come here now to witness this monumental shift, to be fully present and understand the transformation that's taking place and to generate frequency holding patterns for the birthing of a new era; what does your soul feel?

Our planet's Schumann frequencies reveal that we are indeed living at a higher vibration than before. Furthermore, many long hidden secrets are being exposed from many avenues which are getting more reach as each day passes. We are learning the truth about many aspects of our lives that we have taken for granted on so many levels; there is a skyrocketing global awareness of many nefarious plots and plans. Let us continue this transformational journey and see what can be shared with you to fill in some gaps in the unravelling plan.

Origins and Oligarchs.

Is it personal that we are being targeted? The life paths that we have been sold has too many of us living very unfulfilled lives, making our way paycheck to paycheck (if we are among the lucky ones) and this is what we are told to aim for, and as long as we obey and keep paying the exorbitant taxes everything will be just fine, is this really what our spirits were destined for?

There are 144,000 base DNA pairs; DNA is the biggest data storage known to man and this is the the place that all your biological information is held for accessing innate abilities, but 95% of the information storage capacity is yet to unlock and activate, and that is labelled as 'junk or dormant DNA' In practical terms the beginning of the DNA sequence must know the end and everything in between simultaneously, making it a quantum element of you. Using Shungites' access to fullerenes to keep your DNA in tiptop condition is simply a great idea.

Michael Behe, John Lennox and Steven Meyer are three leading voices in science and academia who support the idea of an intelligent designer of the universe and everything within it, including us. The notion of Darwin's evolving DNAs is expertly discredited by these scholars when discussing the topic.

Professors Michael Behe (biochemist), John Lennox (mathematician; with three doctorates) and Steven Meyer (geophysicist) have shown that the time for each amino acid to evolve through the 'trial and error' method of evolution doesn't match the geological records of humanoids on Earth. We simply 'evolved' far too quickly to fit the evolution model. They assert that the 'big bang' theory doesn't account for the miraculous nature of human creation or explain our origins at all. Whilst it's not necessary to know the complexities which are far too detailed for this book, what is vitally important to ponder on are these considered thoughts of a few of the most talented minds on the planet today.

Together they have thrashed out the issue to an expert degree and the outcome is imperative to your understanding of just how special you really are. For example if unwound and tied together the DNA strands in just *one* cell would stretch almost six feet but be only 50 trillionths of an inch wide. If you were to line up *all* the DNA in your body from end to end it would span over 600 trips to the sun and back! This is the equivalent of 100 trillion times six feet times by 93 million miles X1200, (taking the sun's location as the distance from Earth as taught by mainstream science as 93 million miles or 149 million kilometres). The basis of the issue is to consider this; your DNA is incredibly perfect, if there were the slightest deviation of even just *one* protein or amino acid out of this inconceivably long sequence this would simply render your birth an impossibility, which means that you are 'perfect' and that somehow we have arrived as humans in a perfectly completed and inconceivably complicated way.

Darwin's theory of 'evolution' portrays us as 'clever monkeys' but this is simply incorrect as secret Russian scientist Dr Konstantin Korotkov asserts that we were created perfectly as 'light beings' with the ability to influence our environment. He argues that we are not related to apes as Darwin's theory suggests. Whilst Darwin's later published research that walks back this earlier theory, not many people are aware of this or have considered its implications on what it means to be divinely designed, of which we have truly been denied the knowledge.

David Wilcox explores the topic of 'instant evolution' extensively, covering a range of animals that have popped up in the fossil record with no genetic ancestor that they have evolved from, this topic is now being explored and published more mainstream these days too, there is still the case that humans 'missing link' to apes is still *'missing'*. The instant evolution events also cluster in the fossil records every 26,000 years and we are now on the cusp of the next event.

With increasing evidence pointing to the intentional design and creation of the physical world it's a good time to recognise the spark of divinity in each of us; are we about to experience something entirely wonderful that only happens every 24,920 years to be precise? Did you come to this particular place in time to witness something wonderful?

To truly comprehend that each of us has the ability to feel uniquely perfect in our creation can naturally lead us to connect with our Creator, with an invitation to reconnect to something much bigger than ourselves, have we ever considered this before? Who is waiting patiently for us to realise we were made so perfectly? In the water's reflection of their image.

What frequency does all this knowledge open up in each of us?

Is this one of the vibratory keys we must be distracted from finding? What will these thoughts and emotions unlock? It's imperative to truly understand just what a quantum miracle your own creation is.

> *"The goal of the Creator is for each entity to make a conscious choice to again seek Oneness, out of our own free will - not because anyone else forced us to. If we are told what to do and what to believe, then we have learned nothing and will not make any progress. Perhaps the single most basic realisation to make is that we live in a loving Universe.*

> *If we are all One Being, then it is foolish for us to hate anyone, as we are only hating ourselves."*
> David Wilcock

Welcoming in the maker who is waiting, wanting and ready to be a part of our experiences can unlock limitless possibilities, our wanting, longing and yearning for something else, the next 'must have' to fill the loneliness, and with it our neediness gently dissipates when we are able to make these deeper connections and reflections on our divinity. People have joyously exclaimed and relayed stories of this fulfilled spiritual loving experience, explaining that Shungite has been an integral element in bringing them closer to their inner dwelling Godly experience and yet others have claimed that God has simply guided them to Shungite for its healing qualities.

As we reflect back on there being a higher intelligence with us whilst we are experiencing our free will life on planet Earth, given the opportunity we are capable of, many worldwide beneficial accomplishments and great insights that can shape the future for every single one of us is attainable. Recognising the spark of divinity within each of us is crucial, but let us make that more personal: I am and you are the reflection of the intelligent waters of Creation, the silence we experience can feel lonely and isolating until we make an effort to connect and establish our rightful reconnection channel simply by asking to be connected; then we become 'As Kings'

By comprehending that your glass of pure Shungite cleansed water will be reunited with the water spirit that you are, there is much comfort for your being is completed and there is a ripple of joy in your soul.

4

The Hidden Histories

Are those in control today the last of those who have inherited a hijacked and manipulated Cathar like religion; or is there something much more subverted that we should be looking for? What role does Shungite play in uncovering the truth?

Taking a closer look at history, we can draw some parallels between the uprising against governmental tyranny and control by the arrival of Jesus and the current situation we find ourselves in today. Jesus stood for the overturning of megalomaniacal control and was promoting a direct and personal, internal communication with a Creator God, which was also going against the Jewish laws at the time, on one level it's as simple as that.

Rather than relying on a paid intermediary like a rabbi or priest to make moral laws, as well as the heavy handed Roman rules and exorbitant taxes required to be paid to the governing authorities, thus the requirement for pouring money into corrupted systems, synagogues and churches at the behest of the ruling elite which was common sense then the same as it is now. These ideas and his documented miracles combined with his journey touching the hearts of the common people which he stood and died for had such a profound effect on the people at the time who were being oppressed that they also laid their lives down to follow his example, and many hundreds of thousands were murdered by the rulers' forces after him. It came to a head 300 years after Jesus' death, during the reign of Emperor Constantine who reversed the trend of killing Christians and in a complete surprise move becoming the first emperor to 'convert' to Christianity.

However, before his conversion Constantine persecuted specific groups of Christians and the Roman authorities saw the developing new Christian faith as a major threat to their empire because of the sheer number of new converts who were renouncing the Romans' rule. Constantines' convenient flip helped spread the new religion by funding Christian church building projects, commissioning new copies of the Bible, which allowed for a major rewrite and edit which took 28 years to complete, by summoning councils of theologians to hammer out the religion's doctrinal kinks and leaving out a lot of valuable teachings including those that are now known of such as Enoch and Thomas. One such example of subtle but significant editing can be found when comparing the later King James version to the Geneva version from 1560, as importantly the 'worldly governors in high places' are stated as being the prince's of darkness in Ephesians 6 verse 12 and this was omitted by King James along with all 15 books of the Apocrypha.

It's important to note that the new Roman rulers were a combination of Mithraic worshippers mixed with offshoots from the Jewish establishment, simply swapping sides attaining the goal of the continuation of power. By the looks of it they had used the uprising against their tyrannical ways as that of a 'spiritual birthing' and necessary societal reset to grab more power and exert more tyranny in the process, causing even further division; what can a nation do when they are subjected to more tyranny?

There are astounding parallels between the tales written about Mithras, Jesus, and ancient Zarathustra and it's difficult to untangle the threads of information on each one so let's look at the similarities, these include all three being celebrated as born of a virgin (which refers to being unmarried) in a cave on December 25th but this would have been impossible for the journey of Mary and Joseph at that time, as the mountain pass would have been closed with snow. The worshippers of Mithras held strong beliefs in a celestial heaven and an infernal hell, and believed in a final day of judgement in which the dead would resurrect, and a final conflict that would destroy the existing order of all things to bring about the triumph of light over darkness.

Constantine moved the holy day to be in line with his Mithraic beliefs which is Sunday instead of the Sabbath which is Saturday. He even ordered the sacred texts of the apostles of Jesus to match the number of apostles of Mithras which are 12. These newly reworked texts have led to that which we have now, but what of the original texts and teachings, who would know that there were any originals that have been hidden? Has the reworked holy text been altered to support their ruling ethos in any way and in what ways have we been denied the original knowledge?

The control of the masses must be harnessed, and if you can't beat them, join them! Constantine executed a devious plan and buried the religion of the Roman Army officers who were worshipping in underground temples to 'Mithras' the 'god of contracts' into lower level worshipping and sacrifice spaces. His 'conversion' looks like it was the perfect cover up and created the illusion required to keep the empire intact; keeping hold of the reigns, ruling the people of the whole of the Roman Empire as far as it stretched with statues to Mithras being hidden in plain sight today as the 'lady of Liberty' is not a 'lady' at all but is the Masonic nod to ancient Roman rule.

Mithras, Persian god of Light and Contracts. Altars found in a 3rd-4th century AD stone temple near a Roman fort along Hadrian's Wall at Carrawburgh, England details the same rays of light protruding from his head as the 'Lady of Liberty'

The Masons Trans-agenda Idol Donated to America by the Masonic French sculptor Frédéric Auguste Bartholdi

Construction photos - the face can be seen to be masculine.

Discoveries in London and at Hadrian's Wall reveal that newly constructed Christian churches were built directly on top of Mithraic temples. These multi storey structures provided entry for everyone through the same door, allowing the ruling class to secretly continue their Mithraic religion in the lower levels whilst Roman subjects 'Christians' worshipped above. Mithras worshippers, who were exclusively male, underwent seven initiation stages before being accepted into the cult. The initiations, which required participants to be nude and blindfolded, emphasised the importance of secrecy within the group and remarkably mirror the modern Masonic rituals.

His conversion ensured the massive empire's income was secured, as the massacre of huge amounts of his nation's taxpayers would have financially crippled his regime. Eventually he made the persecution of his new 'Christian' followers illegal by signing the Edict of Milan in 313 AD, yet there was a sect that saw this for what it was, and they kept loyal to the original teachings, they were called the 'Cathars'. For the majority of the populace it was safer to convert to Roman Catholicism, with Constantine's ability to unite the masses under one 'Cathar like' religion he could stop massacring his paying nation. By seizing control and quelling dissent Constantine and his new 'Cathar like rulers' turned their attention to the nonconforming pagans.

In 391 AD Emperor Theodosius banned all pagan rituals and sacrifices including the Olympic Games following his rise to power; he consolidated his power by issuing a series of edicts after Gratian's murder by his own troops and there we have the divide, where once common people would have stood together against ruling oppression it was made to be about beliefs.

The Cathars, also known as the Albigenses, were a devout group that believed spiritual fulfilment could also be attained from within, without the need to pay the governmental controllers exorbitant taxes either; they knew the state sanctioned religious teachings were subverted teachings and they swore to keep to the original and directly inspired teachings and journey of Jesus's life, death and importantly his miracles alive. Subsequently they were hunted and massacred for 25 years by the Roman Empire after Pope Innocent III ordered their persecution for not going along with the new doctrines. This persecution was an attempt to quell the rapidly growing dissent against the newly established Roman Catholic Church and lessen establishment overreach by the ruling state. Despite this, the Cathars were able to flourish in Britain due to its remoteness from the main hub of the Roman Empire. According to Graham Phillips's book

'The Search for the Holy Grail' these independent and courageous souls were actually the majority of the population in England. Would that not be a great topic to study in history or religious studies at school?

The Tarot deck has been found to be the original Albigensian teachings in pictorial form, created to aid the memory in retaining key facts and spiritual teachings through the tales of the main character 'Parsifal or Perceiver. The name Parsifal, which is a respelling of Percival, means 'pierce the valley' and refers to someone moving straight through the middle. Parsifal is a reflection of Jesus, initially portrayed as a young fool who eventually enters the castle. As he interacts with the maiden, knights, kings and queens, he eventually finds his way to inner wisdom finally realising how to question, which reconnects to the everlasting waters of knowledge and the Divine presence of the Creator. This is the key to unlocking deeper guidance and true inner insights that can lead a spirit's development through the maze of reality back to the Creator and safely home again after this life. As you ask - you will be answered.

This age-old title has many spelling variations that appear across Welsh mythology and Arthurian legend. Thomas Aquinas references the use of these teachings in southern France during the thirteenth century. The chalice is believed to be both the book of wisdom in the form of the Tarot and the small carved stone cup passed down from Owain Ddantgwyn, the true King Arthur (actually of Shropshire). Later the carved stone cup was discovered to be in the Roman town of Viroconium where Oraphim's Cassie and Rich have followed the journey to uncover this fascinating lost history.

The retelling of the wonders performed by the most famous miracle maker in history are still relevant to this day as in the Gospel of Thomas which is one of the omitted texts from the Bible it states

"Let him who seeks until he finds, when he finds, he will become troubled when he becomes troubled, he will become astonished, and he will rule over all." By our seeking nature we will find our inner kingdom but when we are indoctrinated instead of inspired by teachers and lessons/history/science which have been altered by the ruling class we will be enslaved in both heart, mind and spirit. When we perceive miracles and imagine them they become our reality, is this why Jesus said that we would become better than him, what we think is possible is only limited by our imagination.

Why is this important to Shungite? There are a number of culminating factors to consider; one being because the case can be made for the continued divide, conquer and control of the working classes to this very day, 'modern slavery' is embedded in the fabric of reality with the illusion of freedom. The need for our compliance willingly or unwillingly does not matter to the masters of manipulation; two of the major opposing forces to these controllers have their roots in Russian history, the current sanctions imposed against Russia directly impact the availability of Shungite at this time. With a mass disinformation campaign to discredit the Russian people and its leadership's actions to free the Donbass region's people who had democratically voted to be independent having suffered directly from the abuses of the Ukrainian regime with reports of huge amounts of people and children trapped in human trafficking operations in the Ukraine.

The front men for this cabal of control can be openly identified as the political classes in cahoots with the Monarchy but they are still lowly ranked as they are controlled by the visible Rockefeller and Carnegie families with their control of Blackrock and Vanguard, but again these are controlled by a more invisible upper Elite layer consisting of an even more secretive family called the 'Payseurs' and the Christian counterpart to these Elites being the hidden families of the Merovingians and the Romanovs. The Merovingians' who are identified as the descendants of Jesus Christ who in turn are directly connected to King David, with a strange twist in the current lineage as the trail has been linked to President Donald Trump and his wife Melania who is a surviving Romanov. What will these people in power do to assist humanity living and surviving today?

These layers of visible and hidden rulers are exploiting humanity to further their own greed and objectives, resulting in greater division and chaos, the upsurge of a common sense uprising and spiritual awakening has been suppressed as we are poisoned by toxins in many ways each day by imposed tyrannical regimes who simply govern via fear, coercion as well as divide and conquer tactics and with modern psychological tactics and cognitive dissonance it's simply a minefield of fear and control again. Knowledge is power and your compliance is key.

Do we need a 'Nanny State' to take our time and taxes, to demand our life force energy every day and subservience until we are decrepit in body and subdued in spirit, literally lost souls in a maritime commercial sea? Is that what we came here to experience or to battle and win for once and for *ALL*?

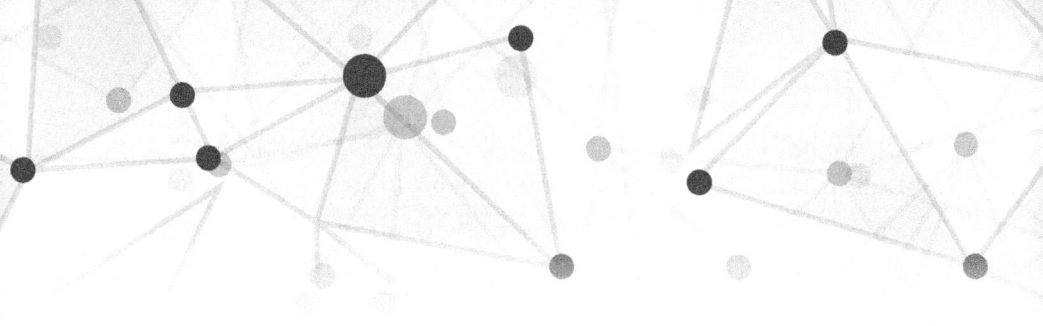

5

Have We Been Denied The Knowledge?

It seems as if the apocalypse is very much here; the word 'Apocalypse' comes from the Greek language, the original language of the Book of Revelation; it means 'uncover, disclose, reveal', and the fight for good over evil is a fight for your soul every moment you are alive.

During Rich's unexpected trip to Scotland having been dismissed from his hospital work of 15 years after his whistleblowing exposed some potentially harmful ingredients in vaccines at the time and had shared evidence that the 'Swine Flu' was a trial run for what we see happening in the more recent past, he experienced an extraordinary event that affected the fate of our planet. He had a near death experience (NDE) where he found himself in front of a vast council of souls that stretched back further than he could see. Rich pounded his fist in desperation, shouting, *"They have been denied the knowledge!"* From the council of galactic nations gathered there, he received his response, *"Thank you for reporting back, you may now return"*; with that his task was complete.

Rich vividly remembers his journey back to his earthly form, he had already passed by the giant sentinels who protect the quarantined earthly realm. He witnessed the narrow band of green energy that supports life on our planet and the diminishing bolts of spiritual lighting connecting through each of us, from the earthly surface to the outer heavens. Each body and soul is a conduit for grounding this life force energy, but the dwindling inner kingdom development of each of us during our modern lives and the introduction of rubber soled shoes blocks our connection to higher realms and this divine energy transference.

Although Rich returned to his earthly form, a part of him remains anchored in that other realm. He now has a gift for bringing through healing music to aid us in our earthly experience. This gift is directly connected to his NDE.

What topics have we been denied the knowledge on; is it our true origins, ancient history, available technology, that we may not be alone in the universe, or something else?

The recent release of information on US 'alien contact' is filling many with excitement; will it aid in filling in some missing links in human developmental history and release subverted knowledge as well as suppressed technology that could revolutionise life here for mankind? Even the Bible has accounts of alien spacecraft that took Ezekiel for a trip as recounted by J F Blumrich who was a major NASA engineer who tried to debunk it but could not.

With the realisation of your true essence as a divinely created being, with innate abilities to profoundly shape your own reality, and be a part of the creation of a world that is beautiful to experience, making it the absolute best we can imagine for each other *is* what we came here for, the fact that there *is* something very valuable inside you, is key knowledge, don't ever overlook it.

If not decided by you, your soul is up for being bought by modern distractions. When we have the basic needs of shelter, heat and sustenance covered, we can make better moral decisions and not be so easily corrupted or swayed by government and control agendas to make bad moral choices that bring harm to each other. You can think for yourself and become AS KING of your destiny. Why is 'asking' so important and what can we learn from these past 'hidden' histories?

The Struggle for Control and the Importance of Healing and Unity

Many cultures throughout history have lost everything and been left with only the clothes on their backs if they were fortunate. This time round the culling is taking place as the AI systems are gearing up to replace human jobs very rapidly. This raises the question of religious relics and the accuracy of spiritual 'Gnosis' teachings. Is it possible to ever truly know the truth when everything gets lost in translation and altered through Chinese whispers; what exactly do we inherit from one generation to the next?

The first and second World Wars in the modern era have resulted in mass migration, loss of life, property and knowledge, and with this inability to pass on much, if anything as an inheritance to future generations whole nations were prevented the growth of personal wealth and power. It's as if entire communities are wiped out in a coordinated manner, and with each technological advancement, a significant portion of the population becomes redundant. Now we are on the cusp of another redundancy revolution with the rise of AI as scarcity is promoted as the cause for a need for depopulation agendas we are left questioning our role here as humans once again.

The pervasive and longstanding systems of control affect all aspects of society, leaving the working classes to struggle for their basic needs whilst being bombarded by pollution from all sides. In this challenging reality Shungite offers a powerful solution to cleanse, heal and elevate the planet to a higher frequency. However, to truly eradicate tyranny and create a new reality, we must unite and envision a better future for each other. To lighten the journey Cassie has invented a game called 'Your Topia' The Winning of the Game depends on our success to imagine together the Dissolving of the Government!

This game builds family and friend's frequencies by directly making beautiful memories without screens or modern tech and incorporates the famous quotes of many past and present inventors which also include August Krogh a Danish Nobel prize winning zoologist who was a prominent scientist and inventor and who was also a cousin of Cassie's great grandmother.

Each player imagines and draws a special invention that will change the World forever and they work their way around the spiral board until they reach the launch pad. Along the way the government tries through tyrannical means to scupper their journey and their success. It includes a range of fun and inspiring activities and some Shungite solutions too; it's focused around the power of our imagination and engaging each other through laughter, fun and powerful desires to help each other. With the ability to utilise your thoughts and knowledge to join together and to activate our hearts desires to create a different reality to the one we were born into. Be a game changer; together we can change the world for each other.

6

The Rise of Shungite in the Age of the Industrial Revolution

Once many many moons ago Shungite was only known about among the Sami tribes of the frozen Finnish regions, but it was discovered to have enormous potential during the dark ages and for Shungite the breakthroughs started to emerge in the Victorian age; whilst the era was characterised by social control and brutality, the Industrial Revolution began with the utilisation of our Earth's blessed water and the implementation of steam instead of human labour. It's important to note that during this time a factory or pit owner valued a donkey more than a human life, and it's not changed that much today, as the governmental operatives and those above them have very little regard for its sovereign souls and this is being exposed even more by the UK C_vid enquiry.

In the mid 1750s James Watts made significant interventions in the separation of hydrogen and oxygen elements in water, which led to the full utilisation of steam power, thus liberating the populace from cheap back breaking labour. Watts also coined the term 'horsepower' as a unit of energy, which helped to conserve 80% of fuel consumption at the time.

Around the same time the agricultural lifestyle gave way to the Industrial Revolution Peter the Great founded the Russian Academy of Sciences and the Saint Petersburg State University in 1724. Some believe that Peter the Great's mother's Tartar features connect to the hidden 'Tartarian' civilisation. The concept of Great Tartaria as a lost civilisation that originated in Russia has gained traction over recent years. Evidence of an advanced way of life with its grand architecture and free energy being derived from the Aether sadly are often dismissed as a wild conspiracy theory. However, one must question why there is a coverup and such a massive tearing down of their old buildings if there is really nothing to hide?

During his reign as a Russian Emperor Peter the Great implemented the old fashioned Julian calendar, he also knew of a small village in the neighbouring country of Finland named 'Shunga', with its healing waters that had saved his own exiled grandmother, Xenia Romanov from the brink of death. Tsar Boris Godunov had exiled her from 1601 to 1606, and she was imprisoned in a tower located in a churchyard behind the village of Shunga. Despite this dark history the village eventually became a thriving marketplace for trade during the 1600s.

Peter the Great had learned about Shunga's very special water with remarkable healing properties and quickly sent a research team headed by physician L Blumentrost to investigate. With their significant findings Peter the Great established the first healing spas for local copper smelters, soldiers and even himself, as he recovered from injury using the black stones in just three weeks. So, impressed with the discovery and the stone's abilities Peter the Great introduced Shungite into the army's water containers for purification during their campaigns. This proved to be a strategic advantage during the 1709 'Poltava Campaign' of the Great Northern War between Russia and Sweden, which ended in victory for the Russians when an unusually hot and humid period produced large blooms of bacteria in the water supplies that infected the Swedish army.

Shungite stones also called 'Viper' stones at the time were so inspiring and healing that on the 20th March 1719 Peter the Great established the 'Marcial Waters' or 'Mars the God of War' Resort in Karelia. He declared *"This water cures various cruel illnesses, in particular: scurvy, morbid depression, gall, stomach weakness, vomiting, diarrhoea, stones, kidneys, and has great power against other illnesses."*

When 'Viper' Stones is popped into a gematria calculator some very interesting results come up such as 'Bigger Better Stronger', 'Eternal Healing Frequencies' 'Unearthly' and 'Yahway'

From 1323 until the 1800s, Finland and Sweden had exchanged ownership of the land; despite the Finns retaining ownership until 1944 when the USSR recognised the region's abundant mineral resources and claimed it as their own; this included the valuable Shungite deposit, which was obtained after two gruelling battles resulting in a loss of 100,000 lives during the 'Winter War' (1939-40) and the 'Continuation War' (1941-44).

In 1812 after the discovery that Shungite powder was stopping the metal gun casing from rusting by the Alexander Cannon Factory in Petrozavodsk, the entire Russian Navy ships hulls were being coated in Shungite, this had been inspired by the first scientific study of Shungite by Nicolai Yakovelevich Ozeretskovsky carried out in 1792, noting that locals would grind it up for use as an ink as well as fertiliser for crops.

Shungite has been utilised in international trade for centuries with diverse applications. For example, British hemp manufacturers used it to line their hemp to prevent cockroach infestations, whilst the Vikings provided the French with Shungite to supply Germanic women who believed it prevented infections during bathing.

Professor Alexander Alexandrovich Inostrantsev (1843-19) was a well known researcher and academic who officially named the incredible mineral 'Shungite.' His research led him to the modern day villages of Tolvuya, Shunga (from which it received its name), and Vozhmozero, where it is primarily found. The Academy of Sciences of the USSR was established which sparked an influx of scientific interest in Shungite. The Academy of Sciences of Karelia led much of this research since Shungite is exclusive to this region with notable researchers publishing on the topic:

- Professor Inostrantsev - 'The newest member of the group of amorphous carbons' 1877

- Professor Inostrantsev - 'More about Shungite' 1886

- Pyotr Borisov - 'Karelian Shungites' 1956

- V Sokolov and Y Kalinin - 'Shungites of Karelia and ways of its comprehensive research'

- V Sokolov and Y Kalinin 'Geology of shungitonous volcanogenic sedimentary formations of the Proterozoic period in Karelia' 1975;

- V Sokolov and Y Kalinin- 'Shungite - 'The new carbon material," 1984

- V Sokolov - 'Radio-shielding properties of composite materials based on Shungite rocks and its compounds' 1990

The Rise of Shungite in the Age of the Industrial Revolution

Oraphim are avid researchers of the latest findings on Shungite, and there are just too many enquiring and publishing that are engaged in Shungite and fullerene research now to keep up.

When we look up the exact day Peter the Great decided to officially open the first Shungite healing spa 'Marcial Waters' 'Mars the God of War' Resort in Karelia it was a new moon on the 'White Lunar Worldbridger' on the modern version of the 'Law of Time' calendar. We all have frequencies that guide our personality traits, most commonly known are the heavenly bodies that are consulted in the astrological divination practices of 'horoscopes', but there is an astounding link between the Pleiades and us via the Mayan 13 moon calendar, which has a modern iteration called the Law of Time Dreamspell Calendar, which links directly and exactly to the passage of Sirius B around Sirius A.

The galactic signature for this special day is:

> I polarise in order to Equalise,
> Stabilising opportunity.
> I seal the store of death.
> With the Lunar tone of Challenge.
> I am guided by the power of Endlessness.
> I am a galactic portal…..enter me.

This can be interpreted as a day that the galactic frequencies aligned with Shungite as it can be identified as bringing great balancing qualities for everyone, the birthing of a new era is also represented by the seal of death, with Shungite being the agent of change for eternity for everyone as it's job is endless, it's the perfect day for launching the spa.

Peter the Great's personal galactic signature based on his birth date 9th June 1672 is:

> Yellow Planetary Human:
> I perfect in order to influence
> Producing Wisdom
> I seal the Process of Free Will.
> With the Planetary tone of Manifestation.
> I am guided by the power of Universal Fire
> I am a galactic activation portal...enter me.

Great leadership values are associated with 'yellow human' galactic frequencies, they are deeply concerned with the balance of right and wrong and free will choices, leadership is about making great changes and seeing how situations can be made better, working towards a goal of perfection with great drive and passion and being fired up to bring much abundance for the people of their nation, with his opening of the Shungite spa to create perfection in healing water he manifested this opportunity for many of his people and beyond to experience.

Today it is interesting to compare this to Vladimir Putin as he is also a 'yellow human' on the law of time calendar (7th October 1952):

> Yellow Resonant Human:
> I Channel in order to Influence
> Inspiring Wisdom
> I seal the Process of Free Will
> With the Resonant tone of Attunement
> I am guided by the power of Flowering
> I am a galactic activation portal...enter me.

Interesting parallels between Putin and Peter the Great are that with them both being world leaders and both being Yellow Humans their focus on wisdom and free will is in sync. These are dominant and strong guiding principles to the way they lead. Peter the Great started the Shungite revolution and in his frequency signature he has manifestation, and Putin seems to be the completer as he is guided by flowering but what is he bringing to an end? Is it linked to the freeing of people of the Donbass region including children who were born into communities trapped in areas of the world plagued by organ and human trafficking that was impacting on their 'free will'?

Exploring the Galactic Frequencies with the Dreamspell App

The Dreamspell App makes it easy for anyone to explore the galactic frequencies. These frequencies can be utilised to accomplish tasks, the hardest things to achieve can be experienced as easy in the right frequency as it lines up on the correct day, connecting with vibrations that align with universal energy, this modern version was developed by founder Jose Arguellles with Valum Votan. Even those who struggle with organisation and being tidy can find motivation and order with the right frequency. Keep in mind that white worldbridger days symbolise the end of old cycles and the beginning of new ones. It's fitting that on the Day of Endlessness, Shungites' infinite spinning C60 fullerene quantum energy is released through the galactic activation portal day.

7

Soul Development - Shungite the Personal Old World Rule Breaker

Whilst Shungite has a growing reputation for personal and spiritual development and overall health enhancements and it is becoming more well known, it sits in a category all of its own unlike any other mineral or crystal form that it can be compared to. Even in the scientific world it had to be put in its own category and is now classified as 'The Third State of Carbon', because whilst it is 'carbon' still and similar to graphite, diamond and coal it does not behave like them enough to be placed in their category. It breaks their rules and it, like you, is completely unique; it does not belong to anything else on the entire planet either.

Shungite can be a powerful tool in transforming negative patterns of behaviour releasing deep shadows for those who have them still to work through, with our 'free will' to experience on this planet have we come here to develop our souls? As the results can be astounding, ranging from subtle changes to complete transformations. Witnessing this inner work unfold over the years has shown that Shungite can get to the roots of shadow negative patterns, bringing them to light for release. However, reprogramming responses and releasing shadows may disrupt the status quo of relationships, maybe this is why the blue glowing ball exploded over the Shungite in Karelia to bring great changes at this time and to raise the frequency so we can see what needs to be reviled; in some cases on a more personal level individuals may need to be completely alone to emerge transformed, others who are aware of this process say it's not a stone for sissies! So do be gentle with yourself when you are releasing illusions and past negative programming, trust that you will emerge the beautiful butterfly you were always destined to be.

Shungite aids in experiencing inner balance, peace and the powerful release of negative emotions which can be life changing, bear this in mind as it can be a bumpy ride transitioning to completely different mental states, especially if someone is trying to hold on to illusions and old states of being. Programming which has travelled down through generations from negative influences or traumatic experiences may have created many manipulative responses and it is a courageous thing to complete the reprogramming task, but maybe this is why you are here now, the results are revolutionary and you can be lifted out of trauma and heal your family lines in both directions.

With Earth being a freewill planet we still have an ability to choose how we play out our interactions and influence their outcomes down here, try to experience the positive difference before choosing or slipping back into old patterns. Observing the spirits of trauma travel down through generational lines and gaining the courage to heal and release a family trauma spirit takes great courage but the benefits are astounding for the person who releases it as well as for the wider family seven generations in both past and future directions. Shungite is here to assist in the freeing of humanity on many levels should you wish to accept the challenge.

A woman who had been subdued by mental abuse during her childhood lived as a quiet and shy adult for her whole life. However, after purchasing a collection of Oraphim jewellery and attending a show a few months later, she expressed her surprise at the positive changes she was experiencing. She even exclaimed that she had become "a little sweary" and was standing up for others in her workplace which was a complete first for her and a positive contrast to her old self.

Imagining from our hearts desires means we must become great at wishing as it can become a reality. Nancy L Hopkins' book 'Cosmic Reality' outlines these laws in their active states. Rule 1 is that reality is what we think it is, and Rule 2 is that the majority rules.

Cosmic Reality Rule 4

"Powerful people keep the masses ignorant in order to control reality. Histories are rewritten and scientific facts are kept as secrets, to prevent individuals from understanding their own personal powers and threatening accepted reality. If each person understood the power of their own thoughts, reality would take on a whole new meaning"

Quantum Alignment with Shungite Grounding

Stepping forward in to a new future by grounding new frequencies and focusing our alignment though this great awakening, whilst learning the horrors of the past and present is a very exhausting experience so having a few tools to help is key, one way is through the ionic transfer of energy between earth and our human body as it is vital for our health and many understand that getting barefooted is essential but not so easy all year round, many studies have shown that when we lose our earth link cot deaths occur more frequently and inflammation in the body reaches epidemic levels.

Shungite creates its connection to our hearts pentagon energy centre which gets activated, cleansed and enhanced powerfully alongside our hexagonal 'grounding' base energy centre that links us to earth, with these inner energy connections being greatly strengthened our desires are aided and amplified, and in swift fashion much positivity can be brought to fruition, this means that grounding is not always a literal connection to earth but energetically accessing our best attributes.

A woman once shared with me that in just three short months of using Shungite she experienced more profound shifts and many more experiences than in her entire life prior. In fact she was off to meditate in the Giza pyramids with a world renowned guru! She had become in alignment with her destiny, she also shared her profound meditation and following dream time experience with her Shungite pyramid which had resulted in being present at a school of Angels, she had joined them in their classroom studying Shungite before they came to Earth.

A powerful world changing activation is to focus on our desires and hold them vividly in our imaginations whilst generating matching emotions then allowing the total release of the thought, this technique is supercharging your 'wishing' and is quantum activating, our lives can become more fluid, with synchronicities occurring more frequently and effortlessly. The transformation can occur even more rapidly when we have the desire and wellbeing of others in our hearts and it's this action that is even stronger when we have silver activated Shungite in our lives. What will you wish for right now, what desire is in your heart for your loved ones?

Personal Trauma and Cultural Healing

Today, many religions, both Eastern and Western, are struggling with the revelations from sexual abuse victims. This has contributed to a decline in faith across society and therefore the decline in the development of an inner kingdom and quiet contemplative practices for many. By understanding our cultural heritage a little deeper we can gain insight into our struggles to get to connect within at a deeper level and we can learn to overcome this once we have the knowledge and see the importance for this inner balance.

Recent revelations have exposed the horrific atrocities committed within many secret sects and societies, with perpetrators including rabbis, popes, priests and priestesses. These groups often employ subverted symbols and rituals, which can now be identified and observed in various public places.

Notably, the Masonic rituals are coming to light to be highly satanic; they also mimic the Mithraic degrees of acceptance and loyalty into their secret order which are limited primarily to males with only recently women's orders setting up. This raises the question as to whether there are genuine sacred texts and teachings which have been hidden and are yet to be unearthed and revealed as so much of the masons influence on modern society is yet to be recognised as satanic.

Many people during the 1960s and 70s turned away from traditional religions and formed alternative cults that had subverted ancient eastern teachings. These groups were often packaged as 'free love' which aimed to discard traditional values and unleash the more conservative 'repressed' sexual spirit, but sadly it is often just sexual misconduct and abuse that is crossing boundaries which the devotees do not understand is happening. Unfortunately, many young men and women who had already experienced inappropriate sexual conduct from past interactions were further damaged by these experiences, leading to new generations of emotionally scarred adults, it is an extremely sad fact that one in four people are being sexually abused today, leading to a myriad of societal and personal problems and this is why we need all the help we can get to bring healing and change society.

This alongside and mixed in with the blooming of the feminist movement in the 1960s which brought about significant changes in responsibilities and changing roles for both men and women, aided by cultural trends and the modernisation of domestic appliances meant that lives were radically changed very quickly. This has resulted in us now experiencing the effects of completely unbalanced appreciation of the sexes and much cultural confusion; the negative programming from past abuses has been deeply embedded and which could take a long time to recover from but without the acceptance of its occurrence we cannot start.

Compounding abuses have left individuals and whole generations altered and damaged, although some of these men and women have emerged from the vale of hidden abuses, they are not always able to create loving and balanced homes because they have not experienced one for themselves; as a result their powerful role as men and women in a positive working family or society is now out of balance. What must we see to heal this division?

Healing the Masculine and Feminine

What we perceive as normal and acceptable needs to be examined, if we are going to embrace new frequencies we need to release old vibrations and stop habits that only hamper our way forward.

It has become increasingly common and is now generally acceptable to publicly mock males at every given opportunity as well as by labelling them as part of the patriarchy. This socially acceptable habit to put down men and belittle them despite their mighty contributions to the physical world they built around us all and that we all rely on, needs addressing and is part of how we need to rebalance our reactions, to value ourselves and others around us is vital to the healing of our current situation before we can move forward successfully together. These old habits must be left behind and our future girls and boys must feel they are divine gifts to us, and that they are perfect in every way; the same way we were divine gifts to our parents once. They must be encouraged to be brought up to surpass us in wit and will and these new generations need loving role models in their parents and they also require an education system to engage their intelligence and inspire them to complete the tasks we have started.

"When Holistic Education is rooted in experiential learning and focuses on the interest of every child, every child is able to take the lead in their own learning. Child led learning takes charge and stimulates not only the child's intellect but also harnesses their creativity and nurtures their spirit."- Ladan Radcliffe (Universal KIDZ)

As we have explored extensively through this book Shungite is doing everything it possibly can to detoxify and heal us physically, to make our frequency uplifted and calm, for us to enjoy the fruits of our personal and spiritual development so that we can connect more strongly and release old paradigms that no longer serve us, aiding to connect with us in a quiet quantum communication, we have all come a very long way and there's still a way to go; Oraphim have researched the work of many ground-breaking pioneers and inventors to be able to develop a few tools to help us take the next steps.

Marsha Burns sums it up succinctly with this wisdom: *"Everything you do in life either lifts you up or tears you down. There are always things that need to be torn down and discarded, but your life is a treasure to be valued and protected."* She concludes by saying, *"Treat yourself with mercy and kindness. You are not your own; you belong to me, says the Lord. Handle yourself with care. 1 Corinthians 6:19-20 or do you not know that your body is the temple of the Holy Spirit who is in you, whom you have from God, and you are not your own? For you were bought at a price; therefore glorify God in your body and in your spirit, which belong to God."*

8

Oraphim Orgone Developments

Wilhelm Reich, an Austrian psychiatrist, conducted research on Orgone energy in the first half of the 20th century, and his findings have paved the way for today's Orgonite devices. Dr Reich discovered that organic materials attract and retain Orgone energy whilst non-organic metals both attract and repel it, hence its reactivating effect on stagnant energy.

Orgone devices are capable of converting dead Orgone (DOR) back into living energy (OR) through the use of crystals. Crystals can align and 'tune' energy through their regular lattice structures, and when added to Orgone creations, they can tune the final frequency. Shungite enhances and directs the flow of energy as well as reading the 'fields' around it, with its quantum intelligence for you to benefit from the connection too, as it links your energy field to the quantum realm.

Shungite's energy from the fullerenes, which spins to the right at least 20 billion times per second, and which has the powerful ability to attenuate toxic frequencies have remarkable effects to be experienced when combined with other Orgonite ingredients. When you add more energy to a closed system, such as our realm this creates what's referred to as 'Time Crystals', this can be experienced and also known as chi or prana, which is a vital force naturally occurring in our lives and working in a focused way is extremely beneficial for many reasons.

Orgonite is a product made of resin, metals and crystals, traditionally balancing and harmonising bioenergy fields by attracting and re-energising dead Orgone. By incorporating the most powerful silver activated Shungite, these multidimensional quantum powerhouses transform into energy activation 'time crystal orgonite' and these have the ability to surpass ordinary orgonite or Shungite working alone. Copper spirals, tensor or Georges Lakhovsky styled metal work are not always necessary in the presence of Shungite's natural energy movement as it's already in the corrected right hand direction, unless used for decorative purposes of course.

Cloud Busters by Oraphim

Hand made in the Oraphim Studios
- Silver Activated Shungite
- Earth Orgone Energy Activation
- Time Crystal Quantum Technology
- Inter-dimensional Bridge
- EMF Busting large scale areas
- Time Line clearing/resetting
- Energy Activation
- Negativity Shifting
- Bio Energy Enhancing
- Networking New Planetary Quantum Grids
- Accessing Higher Frequencies
- Calmer Inner Presence

Cloud Busters are devices that have the capability of transforming a vast area of the environment. During the creation of Oraphim's first cloud buster, Shungite had a unique experience to share. Whilst the metal, crystals, Shungite and poles were setting in the resin outside in the garden, the process's mess and odour prompted the team to leave it outside. At around 2.30 am, Cassie was abruptly awakened by a loud '***CLAP***' from a pair of hands that had startled her awake, but there was only Rich there and he was sound asleep! As she lay awake, she was magically transported to the cloud buster outside, Shungite had a special experience for Cassie that night, to show her just how it does its powerful clearing work.

It did not take long before Cassie saw the earth around her and realised she was in a bubble beneath the cloud buster sitting in the earth somehow. Next, a ring of white light emerged from the cloud buster's base and spread out like a ripple across the surface of a pond taking Cassie with it. She was flying on this band of expanding white light, speeding miles away from the device, until eventually she was transported back to her bed.

This experience highlighted the power of cloud busters, which uses Shungites' white light energy ripple to clear and cleanse the environment for miles, correcting timelines and probably much more. The white light ripple also showed Cassie the nature of 'timelines' in a way that she had not appreciated before, as it clears in a ring, which encompasses the past, present and future.

Oraphim have had other experiences with their cloud busters, one involved the eerie carpark at the retreat centre that needed clearing; initially everyone experienced nausea and dizziness around the device that was placed at the carpark entrance, as if there was a bubble around it spanning about 10 metres. However, after leaving the cloud buster there for a few days, when they returned to the area it now felt 'cleared', and the whole place was bright and fresh with no bubble of nausea at all. The cloud buster had fully released the negative frequencies that it seemed to have captured and quarantined so that the carpark felt light, fresh, clean and calm.

A delighted customer got back in touch to report that after the arrival of their cloud buster she experienced a surge of energy that travelled up her spine and cleared her vision; she ordered a second one, many people have felt the energy connecting with them, grounding them to a deeper connection to earth.

The copper poles are not only polished and varnished for durability but to increase the movement of energy, they are also designed with Oraphims' dichroic designs at the top of the base to add a touch of sparkle in the sunlight. The combination of Shungite activated with silver with black Tourmaline and Quartz in the base is a very powerful combination for working with EMFs, whilst also helping to enhance the quantum energy that is being channelled, creating a powerful biocompatible positive environment and wonderful results.

The Shungite's sentient intelligence has the power to transform the harmful frequency from modern telecommunications into natural sine waves, also clearing airborne toxins resulting in a clear blue sky vista once again as was experienced by Oraphim at their home when they had one sat outside for a long tim;e even a nearby diseased tree was flourishing with healthy leaves the following year, the groundsman for the whole park commenting that the grass was greener and grew fastest around their property.

Testimonial from Jo:

"I got home with my cloud buster and my son, who had been up most of the night, went to bed and said he slept like he hadn't for a very long time

My legs were aching from the inside all day yesterday, it felt as if one healing was happening as I believe I have some chronic issues with my legs, family patterns et al.

I was thinking yesterday that there is a heavy energy in my house, I have felt it for the last few years, I often feel too tired to function properly. I think it affects my son too. I just felt a shift while here on my bed doing my work stuff and catching up, I suddenly felt full of energy and am embodying love!" Jo Leaf

The energy emitted from these devices can travel like a ripple through the aether, covering vast distances as shown to Cassie. Additionally the energy can be focused into a beam that connects with either the human body or other devices in your home. By pairing with other devices that have an electromagnetic field, such as your body, these devices are able to work in harmony with you creating the 'time bubbles' of quantum response experiences for all to benefit from.

9

New Platonic and Pyramid Power

Pyramids are one of the many wonders of the world and as more are discovered we are slowly getting to know that they were not built as tombs for ancient dead Pharaohs. Pyramids have been found in the most unexpected locations. Oceanographer Dr Verlag Meyer, using sonar technology, discovered two crystal-like structures off the coast of Bimini that are three times the size of the Great Pyramid in Egypt. Moreover EMF images of the Giza pyramids reveal that they are drawing in negative EMF frequencies and redirecting them safely into the earth, which is useful to know when we are experiencing the increased number of plasma ejections from our Sun during this latest solar maximum cycle.

The largest and oldest pyramids found to date are in Visoko, Bosnia they match the layout of the constellation of the Seven Sisters - Pleiades, inside the pyramids they have the most remarkable readings for healing negative ions which are causing visitors to report experiences of remarkable healing just from being inside for a few hours; like Shungite stones which are able to pass an electrical current some pebbles found inside the tunnels also mysteriously conduct electricity.

Shungite pyramids can help us shed our old ways, create new desires and align us with positive directions in life. As it activates our energy field and acts as a portal for new quantum transformations to occur through the releasing of trapped / connected frequencies.

- **Grounding Negative EMF Energy**
- **Quantum Cellular Healing**
- **Balancing Bioenergy**

Pyramids can be held with your fingers touching the sides, instantly creating a calm moment to rebalance your energy field.

To activate your energy field, point the tip at your core or someone else's back and moving it in small and very gentle circles to the right / clockwise may result in the 'whoosh' or light headed experience as Shungite takes your frequency into a higher range.

The further away from the body you take the pyramid the different inner development pineal / third eye, glands and energy centres are activated; then memory frequencies, disturbances and negative attachments can be energetically cleared and healed.

- The person holding the pyramid can often feel the excess energy being cleared from the body.
- The body can often feel pulled or pushed forward, centering off balance energy.

- Areas that are 'dis-eased', damaged or causing pain can often experience a warm sensation as the Shungite energy goes straight to them to start healing them.

Resting your hand away from the pyramid for a little while before you very slowly and gently move your palm over the tip, you may feel the energy surrounding it, with a 'little wind' or energy coming from the tip, this is quantum healing energy, aether perturbations of a right hand beneficial spin.

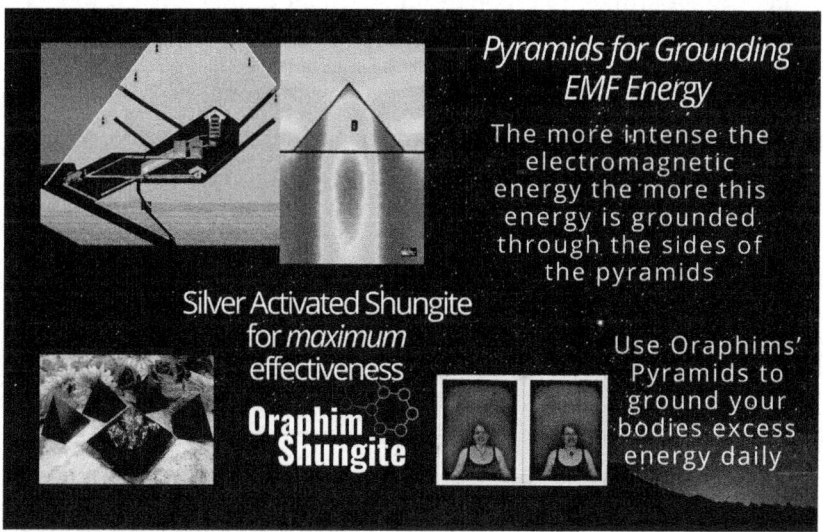

Experimental data confirms that shungite pyramids are a reliable shield against geopathogenic phenomena; these disturbances are formed in nature due to faults in the Earth's crust, underground rivers, mineral deposits, and other unexplained causes. It has been established that if a person is close or within the radius of the geopathogenic zone on a daily basis, their body is invisibly attacked by geopathogenic rays, causing inexplicable malaise, apathy, headache and weakness. As a result, the immune system weakens, disharmony appears, which leads to dis-ease, and the manifestation of diseases becomes more frequent. Medical research shows that geopathogenic radiation causes cardiovascular diseases and up to 60% of cancer diseases. Shungite pyramids are one of the most effective means against geopathogenic radiation as they can reduce the negative impact of the environment, reflect and neutralise geopathogenic rays. A person who is close to the pyramid increases immunity, improves overall health, relieves nervous tension, eliminates headaches, insomnia, and increases tone on their body.

The energy from a Shungite pyramid is different to a Shungite pencil, bead, ball or stone. The pencil and softer rounder shapes have no edges. The pyramid has faces, the energy repeatedly reflected inside the pyramid increases its effect and goes out through its vertices, and we get the energy of Shungite, multiplied by several hundred times. Therefore, the energy from the pyramid as a whole is more powerful than the energy of just Shungite, this is further enhanced by the use of the silver activated Shungite powder.

In Almaty, a town in Kazakhstan, an unusual experiment was conducted on the roads. At one of the emergency intersections of this city, a hundred kilogram pyramid was installed underground, the frame of which was made of ebonite and filled with shungite powder. It's interesting to note that there's a reduction in accidents by 30-35% when empty pyramids are buried in the most dangerous places in Germany and Slovakia. The Alma-ATA pyramid also quickly affected the statistics of road accidents, the number of which decreased by 30%. After this successful experiment, Shungite pyramids were recommended to be taken by drivers as a means of preventing accidents by the Karaganda branch of the road safety Foundation.

These ancient technologies certainly were created by people who seemed to know more than we do now, there is much more we can we learn from the past than we do from the present is seems even with advances in all areas of science, what else is there locked away, hidden information we have yet to tap into, have we been denied the knowledge?

World First: Oraphim Shungite Heptahedrons

Being pioneers in the Shungite creative space has brought beauty to Shungite in ways that had not been done before, and this latest creation by Cassie and Rich is no exception, and it was brought into existence by Alex's asking: "Can you make me a Shungite Heptahedron" and in that moment the answer was "yes". A little while before Cassie's discovery of Shungite she had been creatively exploring the recently discovered 7th platonic solid; her work can be viewed here: https://www.facebook.com/creatorhedron. Discovered by Frank Chester his work gained him recognition as a Nobel Prize nominee, this special shape is intrinsically linked to the human heart and the shape of our planet which he expertly shows via his myriad of mathematically accurate models and the depth of this insights are astounding, this is another fascinating topic that Cassie and Rich have integrated into their inspiring school teaching.

So these are the very first *Silver Activated Shungite Heptahedrons* that have ever been made and many more will be made and released to do the fine frequency shifting work that will assist the coming age to bloom into fruition, as they do indeed bring a whole new vibration when being used to activate our heart energy.

You too can join the countless souls who have experienced the transformational power of Oraphim Orgone devices with silver activated Shungite whether it's with a cloud buster, a pyramid or a pendant.

On several occasions, individuals have reported encountering a 'being' whilst experimenting with Shungite devices. However, the being's face remains concealed. One such encounter occurred during Nancy L Hopkins' remote viewing experience, where she asked to see the origins of the blue object that exploded over Shungite in Karelia just 10 days before the first global pandemic lock-down.

According to Exodus 33:20-23, *"You cannot see my face, for no man can see Me and live!"* We experience the separation from a higher power or being until we reach out or rather reach inwardly to seek that connection, and this lack of connection leaves us feeling isolated and uncertain as we navigate the complex journey of spirits experiences.

There have been instances where others have encountered a beautiful being whilst exploring Shungite and shared their stories, on one occasion a lady holding an Oraphim Shungite pyramid pivoted it to point towards herself, she startled and opened her eyes, Cassie asked what had happened, the lady reported that there was a being, gently observing her, and checking if she was ok, is this the same being that 'clapped' Cassie awake that night to take her to show what Shungite is capable of?

10

Silver Activated Magnetic Shungite Transformations

Magnets themselves are a fascinating area of study just on their own, considering that when one is divided or broken into two pieces the north and south is still present in the two halves and this continues into infinity, so there is no ability to separate the north from the south.

Magnet therapy has been used for thousands of years and it is said that Cleopatra used magnets on her face to help maintain a youthful appearance (as well as daily massage and bathing in Asses milk with scented oils every day.)

Magnets are becoming well known for their energy saving abilities as well as healing qualities with astounding transformations being experienced by combining the silver activated Shungite with the rare earth neodymium magnets which are being explored through the 'Emotional Code Technique'.

By combining amazing silver activated Shungite with neodymium magnets entropical electrical energy throughout your home and workspace is transformed in an extremely powerful way, as evidenced by many with the Shungite silver activated fridge magnets, surprising people who have to turn the dial *up* on their fridges as they are now using less electricity to do the same cooling job as before, and their food is lasting much longer, with reports from avocados not browning, humus lasting a whole month, spinach lasting days longer and raw milk lasting a full 5-7 days. The fridge magnets work by both attaching to the outside or being placed inside if you have a non-magnetic door; and you are also creating a healing electrical device for the whole house as the fridges energy field is not upsetting your energy field any more, but creating a powerful energy enhancing field to your whole home.

Reports have come back to Oraphim over the years of astounding results, including noisy old fridges becoming quiet, gas fridges becoming cold in the height of summer, freezers getting a much deeper freeze and family members becoming more connected to the needs of others and being kinder to one another in remarkable ways.

These fridge magnets can be used to activate the KELEA effect for making fuel in vehicles go further too; simply attach a Shungite magnet to the base of the seat in your car and see how much further you get on your tank of fuel as these have also reported back their astonishing results:

"I was getting 46 mpg before the magnet, now I am getting 52 mpg!" David September 2023

"I love these magnets and have put them on my electrical appliances. I have been monitoring the fridge and as you promised, it is cooler! Thank you so much" Linda 09 September 2021

"Can feel energy in hand! - Petrol consumption noticeably reduced with the Shungite magnet attached to the Land cruiser! Very interesting useful cost effective devices w/ added sparkle!" Steve McCloud 27 Dec, 2021

With the cost of living crisis we are all cutting back and looking at where we can be more economical and environmentally friendly. Oraphim distributed the magnets around a large commercial retreat centre placing them on the heaters, boilers and appliances; the energy bill had been £1100 per winter month the previous year so when the management announced the savings everyone was surprised and very pleased to hear that half was being saved as the bills were £550 per winter month, the Shungite was reducing the heavy consumption of these devices by spinning the electromagnetic fields in line with nature. An additional bonus was experienced as the energy workers delivering their courses also noticed a difference in the centre too 'energetically' everything was getting smoothed out. Easy simple solutions with results from better working appliances using less energy naturally, where will you try yours?

"Safely arrived in carefully package. Straight away stick to my refrigerator; mini trampoline metal legs which I found make me feel lighter when doing my exercises because of the Shungite effect."

Dr Bradley's 'Emotional Code' technique uses muscle testing which is based on working with one emotion at a time to establish the core issue and in which part of the body this issue is lodged, as we discussed earlier that emotions generated find somewhere to go within us. Having established this, the next step is to find out if the issue is personal only to that person in this lifetime or is an intergenerational or a past life issue.

The next step is to use appropriate affirmations to release this trapped emotion whilst using a magnet, running the magnet along the Central Governing Meridian from the top of the lip over the head and down the spine. This swipes the emotion (like a credit card reader) from the cellular memory. For present life issues swipe 3 times, for longer standing issues, swipe 10 times. Then ask the subject to run around and shake the memories off. It may not be necessary to know what the issue is, although in the next few days the subject may remember or sense the origin of the trauma.

Roberta Beer has been exploring the use of the Oraphim silver activated Shungite magnets and is leading the way by combining these two marvellous healing modalities.

Roberta has kindly shared her account "Recently I have been working with Shungite magnets and 'The Emotional Code Technique' to release trapped emotions at the cellular level or bioenergetic level. The results have been astonishing; and I would like to share the following experience with you; I first started exploring this emotional code bioenergetic therapy with a friend, who muscle tested and found that I had anger issues in my gallbladder; I knew intuitively that I had inherited this from my mother and also sensed that this was a generational issue passed down from her mother; I asked my friend to ask if this was to do with mum and how many generations this went back? The answer was five generations!

I then repeated the following affirmation:- I willingly release the anger from my gallbladder and all cells of my body. I let it go, I do not need this emotion any more, it does not serve me and is holding me back from the Abundant Health, Love and Happiness that I deserve.

I then ran around the room, shaking off this stagnant emotion. It was great fun! My friend and I talked and I told her that my mum was beaten by my dad and that I knew that her mother had also been beaten by her husband too, it seems by three grandmothers' in our family! The following day I woke up feeling happy for the first time in many years and also found that I felt more compassionate towards my partner and was able to be with him without falling into passive aggressive mode. The gallbladder issue is significant as I ended up in hospital last year mentally confused with pains in my gallbladder.

I have continued working with this technique on myself and friends, these amazing magnets are powerful Orgone generators and can be used directly on the body, you can use surgical tape to put them on your chakras or areas of pain."

Roberta has a final message to share "Using the magnets has ignited the healer within me and I'm beginning to be ready to serve humanity with this beautifully simple bioenergetic technique. I so much want the Awakened Ones on Earth to release their negative programming, to make way for new beautiful energies of the New Earth, as we step through the Doorway of 2024 together into the New Age of Aquarius and Aquarian Healing. Let us all release all that is holding us back from enjoying Abundant Health, Love and Happiness. This is my prayer." Roberta Beer, Reiki Master/Oraphim Distributor. January 2024

We are likely to be suffering from Collective PTSD from trauma based mind control techniques implemented by the government's C_vid policies of isolation and emotional guilt so this method is useful for all of us to take a moment to clear these most recent energetic disturbances.

Such vibrational changes can have a significant impact on one's life, altering the frequency and thereby changing the timelines of entire families. Olga Kharitidi, a Russian psychiatrist, delves into the topic deeply explaining how ancestral trauma spirits can be passed down through generations and how healing these generational timelines can halt the harm from repeating forward for seven generations.

11

Transitioning Times to Greatness

"You never change things by fighting the existing reality. To change something, build a new model that makes the existing model obsolete."
R Buckminster Fuller

What can we make of this whole situation? What can we do? What will happen to us all?

Many of us are experiencing uncertainty, and moments of fear are natural during this tumultuous time. With the mainstream media remaining mostly silent on the topic of excess deaths and the number of people falling ill is increasing, it's natural to wonder what's going on. Some believe that the world is dividing into two, with talk of 'ascension' and 'soul contracts' and with the proposed 'End Times' others believe that it's the 'Apocalypse' according to the Greek definition, apocalypse means to uncover, reveal, lay bare or disclose.

It's finally time for us to see the reality of the situation as it is unveiled more and more each day. We can fully see the true intentions of those in positions of power who harm the many in a myriad of ways.

By choosing to make the ultimate soul contract to never cause harm for profit or gain and by understanding the implications of our actions, ultimately taking responsibility for our reactions, our souls are growing up and maturing, are we becoming ready to be released into a greater galactic adventure; our nonphysical connections to each other are being made and strengthened each day. Our souls frequencies rising together could well be how we create a new reality and lift out of and above the existing one.

Will we transition to a new level of existence and experience the possibilities that the rest of the galaxy has to offer in our lifetime?

Why has humanity been targeted by its rulers? Is it because we were created by a divine being?

Have our rulers become intoxicated by an evil power and that they are in the process of destroying humanity for this powerful energy they harvest from others suffering, to fulfil some contract they have made with a darker force? Who is Div_c?

Shungite is here to assert our sovereignty in our inner kingdom and give us strength and healing in a myriad of ways. By keeping the questions flowing and not settling for someone else's answer we can continue to learn, grow and discover the answers together; and together we are AS KINGS!

You are a part of the fabric of reality that brings forth by your questions the answers that change reality.

Cassie had prayed for her creative skills to be used to help and heal others and was divinely guided to find Nancy's radio show and work with Shungite and it's quantum connecting fullerenes in a much bigger way than she had before; Cassie's communication with this inner guidance is at times a very active two way conversation as she receives direct replies on many occasions; one such event resulted in her following the direct instructions with this inner beings conversation. She was divinely guided to meet Rich, as she sat for a short while in a Sheffield café on the 10th January 2015, he walked in and she knew this was the very man God had spoken to her about. She had requested help and when a friend had met Rich and was relaying the meeting God told her *"He's the one,"* she had asked for divine intervention in finding her a partner to love and support, as she was recognising that negative patterns were influencing her choices of boyfriends and they were not good choices.

She had reached inwardly asking for assistance, her inner wish was being made real; as during that first magical meeting with Rich they shared their love for research on topics covering art, water and sovereignty and out of the blue he asked *"Are you Cassie?"* *"Yes"* she instantly replied, her heart swelling and her face beaming, he said *"I have been told I have to meet you."*

That very morning on the 10th of January Rich had opened his Angel book at random and read *"Today you will meet the woman who will see you for who you really are."* which indeed had been confirmed by meeting Cassie that day, but it was six months earlier that her neighbours at the 'offgrid community' where she lived the year before who had told Rich of Cassie. He asked Archangel Michael to watch over Cassie and indeed she felt an Angelic presence that following week.

Together they utilise the power of Shungite to deliver their creative talents in service of helping and healing others, this is why they are here together for you now.

Your journey is unique, and what you will experience next is a mystery and a miracle, your questions will light up the world with answers bounding towards you faster than you could have ever imagined. Are you ready for what's going to happen next?

Could Shungite's frequency be uplifting humanity and preparing us for a transformation of biblical proportions?

Quantum Recognition: Instant Alignment with Your Wish

Shungite and its fullerenes have unique properties in the realm of energy creation as we have been exploring through this journey together, the pentagon and hexagon shapes in particular hold special significance; the five sided pentagon corresponds to the Heart Chakra energy centre, which helps individuals generating inspiration, find inner peace and heartfelt healing. Some people may even experience heart palpitations as Shungite really does unblock the heart's energy pathways for healing their heart space allowing new experiences of loving energy, releasing trauma energy or negative conditioning. In divine combination, the six sided hexagon connects to the Root Chakra, making it a powerful tool for seeing the flowering of our desired outcomes, your desires for both you and others are channelled through this Base Chakra connecting to earth and the heavens and the quantum realm, with your powerful imagination and emotions, you are a potent reality maker.

When we create or imagine a specific wish or desire which we then let go of, we begin to witness magic and miracles unfolding in our lives. This may mean more coincidences falling into place, leading us towards our goals. For example, Cassie once wished for Rich to see a crop circle, even though she had never seen one herself. That same night, they arrived at the Rollright Stones in Oxfordshire and the very next morning a woman passing by told them about the crop circles in the field directly next to them. Two crop circles had appeared in the wheat field between the King's Men and the Whispering Knights, one of which was a complex design based on a five-pointed star with a pentagon inside it; they had no knowledge that there were crop circles here at the destination when they set off, yet there they were right next to Rich as he woke up just as Cassie had asked for them to be!

There are a number of theories to be found on the Internet as to the meaning of the designs: a 'golden ratio', 'golden triangle' or kite, night sky astronomy, the image of a 'bird' in the landscape or 'signs on the earth' that foretell the return of Christ. For further information visit: http://www.cropcircleconnector.com/2015/whispering/articles.html

Whilst the meaning of crop circles is open to interpretation and their making rather mysterious in some cases, for Cassie and Rich it is one of those things that they look back on as a sign of integration, with their direct connection to geodomes they were about to work with fullerenes in Shungite. A valuable lesson learnt in that moment was that when making your wish for someone else it speeds up its manifestation, *or* alternatively it can be seen that they were just in coherence with the appearance of the crop circle, and as she was driving them Cassie had simply connected to them in the landscape? The quantum conundrum strikes again as humans are we the antennae for frequencies that we can tune into? The power of not knowing is far more potent than being a boring know it all. Keeping the future open to new answers is enlivening; and simply what joy is to be experienced next round every corner.

12

The Limitless Potential - A Glimpse into the Future

"I just invent, then wait until man comes around to needing what I've invented." "One in ten thousand of us can make a technological breakthrough capable of supporting all the rest."
R Buckminster Fuller

The combination of Shungite and silver may be the exception to the rule, the one that breaks the 'laws of physics' that people often tout as unbreakable. In a world full of limitless combinations and possibilities this metamaterial proves that the impossible is possible. What other technological advancements could be on the horizon?

At Oraphim Cassie and Rich have in their small way already begun to create this different reality for others by exploring the potential of Shungite, in various devices and settings this has heralded a range of exciting results. By integrating Shungite magnets into electrical devices and fuse boards in homes results have successfully boosted efficiency and reduced energy bills. When it was tested extensively at a retreat centre in Derbyshire, the winter electricity bill was nearly halved with an extra £20k in their charity s bank account that was not budgeted for; that allowed for vital repairs the following year. Some that have come to understand Shungite and its fullerenes have seen its potential to revolutionise power generation solutions, providing limitless energy and opening up a world of creative possibilities, in the right hands and with the next generation of minds who meet with this marvellous mineraloid there is a lot to look forward too.

Imagine a future where sustainability doesn't mean depopulation or the depletion of Earth's resources; instead Shungite and its fullerenes will be integral in creating a world where life can flourish in every community.

Building a new Shungite reality is happening all around us. By reading this you are already immersed in its quantum frequency, answering your heart's longing to experience more than the superficial or being a suppressed spirit. Every day is a different frequency to connect with and as the Shungite enhances and aligns your heart's energy, engaging your abilities and hearing your inspired desires, each step takes us deeper into it.

With Shungites' help to ground these healthy desires into reality which we have looked at extensively, into the *here* and *now*, releasing artificial timelines, it soothes your soul so you can experience unexpected moments of calm, allowing you to connect to your inner peace like never before. It's time, you could well be ready and waiting for the expansion of your being, with Shungite giving you energy from the quantum connection that it brings to you, often described as a gentle friendship, a new companion, that sees *you* from its place in the quantum realm.

Your perfect DNA is a spiral stairway imagine now how it leads step by step up each rung to your greater inner kingdom, building this inner land as Umai explains is vital, and which Rich is ready to help people through with his musical healing frequencies (which is whole advanced technology in itself). Only you can make the shift, regarding your body as being a tabernacle for the divine soul to experience this world through our eyes which are the lenses of the spirit, made of water and able to judge the actions of the corrupted rulers *you* are the conduit for the final judgement to take place. As you open your eyes now and are shown their devilish actions.

The fullerenes in Shungite are supporting the very building blocks for our DNA to make the connection between heaven and our earthly existence. Each step on the ladder of our DNA has the very signature of a Divine Creator, now it's a very personal journey, including what name we each give to our Creator being. You have the invitation in your heart and an opportunity to connect with a divine guide in a direct vessel called the 'tabernacle'; we become a witness to the wonders of how everything works out perfectly, especially when we leave a little bit out of our control and at the feet of the Almighty Creator, who provides perfectly in a quantum way, in a way that shows us we were already catered for before we were even aware we had such a need that was being provided for, and in a way that we do not have the capacity to fully comprehend. It is simply wonderful to still find there's much to wonder about.

13

Story Time - Science Finally Catches up with Folklore

As society and science continue to progress, there is a growing desire to reconnect with old ways and nature. As humans continue to feel more disconnected from the earth than ever before, but science is increasingly finding answers closer to nature.

Get ready to delve into the rich folklore of the Sami people, passed down from generation to generation. These tales weave together the ancient mysteries of Shungite with the modern understanding of fullerenes with precise descriptions of their movements mirroring in astonishing accuracy. So sit back, relax, and let's begin the story.

Once upon a time in a certain region of Finland named Karelia, there lived a giant named Valit who had enormous strength but very little wisdom, alongside that he had an extraordinary ability, he could fly. Valit's favourite pastime was finding fresh fish to eat and throwing huge rocks into the numerous lakes situated in the area, which is famously referred to as the 'Thousand Lakes' and the area is also known as the 'Belly of the Earth'. Watching the water splash onto the banks brought him immense delight when he could not find any fish.

Legend has it that one day, in a moment of clumsiness, he slipped and banged his funny bone which he did not find funny at all, up he lept flying high into the sky in a rage. High above the Earth in amongst the stars he stumbled upon a rock with *spinning eyes* which he hurled back down to our planet, where it landed on the earth in the Finnish region.

This origin story has been passed down for hundreds of generations, believed by many to be how Shungite, the very rare and mysterious mineral made its way to earth.

In this book, you have learned that fullerenes are unique atoms formed in perfect geometric shapes that spin with a vacuum inside them, with speeds that connect to other dimensions and that Shungite mysteriously contains every single element on the periodic table and the earliest signs of life have been discovered in the same region; just like a placenta gives all that is needed for a developing baby, Shungite has everything for a developing Earth and our own bodies.

These fullerenes are matching the description of 'spinning eyes' perfectly in the Sámi tribes story of Valit the giant, and with the Hopi tribes tales and prophecies of a mysterious blue meteor which actually came to pass these tales are proving truer than we could have ever imagined.

Did you know that the name 'Valit' which belongs to our giant in Finnish mythology, can be rearranged to spell 'Vital' a word that perfectly captures the essence of Shungite, it's simply: *vital* to us now.

It is important to recognise that you are a unique combination of all the knowledge and research you've acquired in your life so far.

No one else will view an idea quite like you, and every idea you make reality is a tool for your soul's growth, guiding you to explore different places on Earth and beyond and we are all dependent on what each of us brings forth for the development of humanity.

Oraphim believes that embedded experiential learning is essential to helping people feel that they are truly co-creating this transformation, in whatever small part we play in keeping up with the Earth's frequency shift; it's a beautiful team effort and your integral to it, welcome on board special sou; your exceptional emotional intelligence is part of the quantum fabric of our newly shared reality!

There's so many possibilities when it comes to using Shungite, planting your next crops with it, or keeping you and your pets healthy, gifting something for family and friends and using it throughout your home through this earthly transformation, maybe ask for a little inner guidance to get you going.....What transformation will I put into action with Shungite helping? And who's lives will you see it transform?

As it was stated much earlier in this book that it matters what you know and how you feel about it, it can be concluded with information on the energy centres as we combine all that has been shared along this transformational journey. Shungite is able to infuse your energy to bring balance, as your soul manifests itself in various parts such as the spirit body, mental body, energy body, etheric body and physical body that chakras are energy centres but at the same time at the most physical level, it is our glandular system. Every reaction and thought creates emotions which are processed by your glands, and each gland releases certain hormones which are responsible for influencing our energetic, mental and emotional states and vice versa.

For example, when you feel fear or excitement the hormone that is released in your system is adrenaline and the release of this hormone further influences your thought patterns as well as actions and behaviour; but with Shungite reducing your physical stress responses to EMF and Wi-Fi signals that we are bathed in, Shungite is instilling a new general sense of calm and balance, it is a fact that the release of cortisol is reduced and its impacts lessened by having Shungite around. This is how you truly master your chakras, your mind and your energy. The level of emotional intelligence you can unlock with Shungite is remarkable and not only that you will also master your sensitivity too. Your ability to imagine your heart's desires increase. This is a new level of being and mastery and a whole new positive outlook without inflating the ego.

What does powerlessness do to your system?

With the tirade of tyrannical tactics employed by the rapidly failing governments it is easy to engage with feelings of powerlessness as this is completely natural. However, as power is related to the Solar Plexus Chakra or the gland which is responsible for the secretion of insulin and glucagon hormones, which are responsible for breaking down food and converting it into energy, similarly the Solar Plexus Chakra represents power and transformation and can be blocked by shame. Shame is the block that makes one feel powerless; shame that we don't do something to change reality so we don't believe or imagine that anything really can change for the better; which is when we wrongly believe we are insignificant random cells that came about just by chance, then we embody the powerlessness on every level of our being. By changing what we know and how we feel about our origins as a species, we can influence the outcome.

Ultimately the fullerenes vibration is 20-30 billion times spinning to the right which is the enhancing effect of all that is beneficial whilst achieving attenuation and absorption of harmful EMFs, and giving electrons to free radicals to balance, nullify and create more complex structures required by the body intelligently, achieving the balance in the unbalance world; the fullerenes, due to the mysterious vacuum each one has inside its structure, coupled with the torsion field hyperdynamics is pulsing allowing the proto energy from the quantum field to enter our realm, the silver activation process Oraphim does holds the quantum door open and the energy works with the powerful natural electromagnetic fields created by us, to put us into enhanced states and man-made electronics 'waves' in biocompatible states with us.

It is your job to embody the realisation that you're a pure soul being and you are the result of a divine creation and you simply need to embrace this as fact, allow the feelings for yourself to change as you recognise this deeply within, generating healing in your solar plexus, this in turn helps you digest food better and then there will be no more lethargy, procrastination or laziness as you connect to the eternal waters which you are and which will never run dry. These waters which are giving more life force energy enabling us to be world changers, this then mirrors and ripples as an aether perturbation into your environment; all there is to do next is to anticipate miracles for them to appear.

The most important thing to change is the beliefs you hold about yourself, once you have mastered that everything else can vibrate in resonance with your highest frequencies going forward and Shungite is key to accessing and instilling these new states of being.

Whilst it's been a challenge for me as a dyslexic artist it's also been an absolute pleasure writing this to you, but I must get back to the studio to get creative with Shungite and help Rich deliver his healing music wherever it is called for, so the next chapter has to be written by you….As you make your wishes our shared reality and your desires become miracles.

With love and best wishes from

Cassie

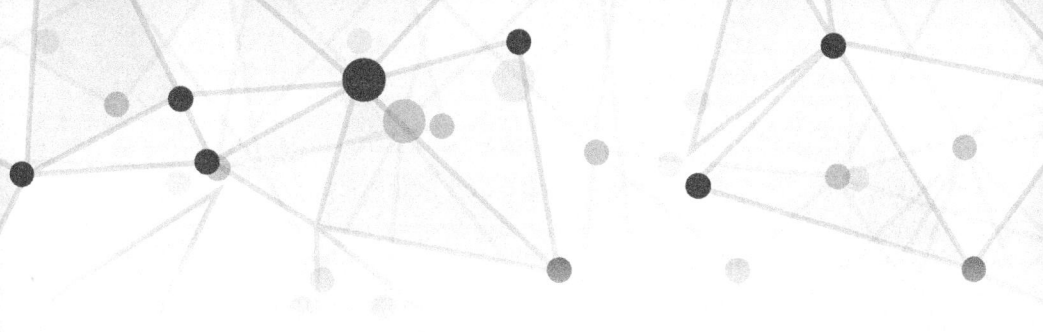

14

Extra Special Shungite Transformations

Countless individuals have experienced remarkable recoveries from various symptoms by incorporating Oraphim Shungite products into their daily lives. In some extreme cases where individuals were wheelchair bound, they were able to resume activities such as gardening and taking walks, effectively improving their quality of life in a miraculous way. The antihistamine properties of Shungite are responsible for repairing the damaged myelin sheath, which is the protective covering of the nervous system. This makes it an excellent antidote to artificial airborne toxins classified as EMFs or electromagnetic frequencies.

By sharing stories from Regina Martino's book Oraphim were able to suggest different ways to use Shungite and this instigated many people to experience similar positive results. Many individuals who have incorporated Shungite into their daily lives have achieved remarkable recoveries and they often get inspired to write these accounts and send them back to Oraphim and a few of these have been included throughout the book, but here are a collection of many more miracles for you to read and be inspired by.

Oraphim received a message from a man with diabetes who had to have his toes amputated due to poor blood circulation. After receiving his Shungite parcel a few days later he made an instant improvement in his ability to relax and sleep as he had not been using any opioid pain relief. When the nurse changed his wound dressings they were amazed to find that his wounds had healed unexpectedly quickly. This was a direct result of the Shungite increasing his circulation, allowing blood to flow to his extremities once again.

A gentleman who had an underactive thyroid for over three decades found the solution he needed by wearing a silver activated Oraphim Shungite pendant. After three months of constant use the wearer's doctor called him in for a routine thyroid function test. To everyone's surprise the physician was able to reduce their Thyroxine prescription by a third immediately. It is important to note that an underactive thyroid is typically considered incurable by the medical establishment and only tends to worsen over time, making this instance even more remarkable.

A Lupus patient experienced a great deal of relief and was able to regain remarkable finger dexterity. After one year she discovered that her need for HCQ usage had decreased significantly, with only one tablet needed per month and has now not needed to take any medication for two years.

Jackie got in touch to report her ganglion had dissipated after about four hours in total of a toggle being placed over her ganglion. The last application resulted in a detoxification headache and then it has now gone. Probably took six applications as the toggle wasn't too comfy on the wrist at that time she adds.

According to a woman who previously suffered from acid reflux her symptoms have been completely alleviated by regularly drinking Shungite water.

Feedback from some parents who had given their children the little tie on bead bracelets said that their children experienced a decrease in allergies from wearing even the smallest silver activated Shungite bracelet.

Gum abscesses below teeth can be a serious concern, potentially leading to tooth loss and significant distress. However, some individuals have found relief by using Shungite powder mixed with water to treat the infection. Simply swirl the mixture around the infected area, spit it out, and leave the remaining powder on the area overnight. In most cases the infection is cleared by the following day.

Medical studies at a Belgorod region sanatorium found that a Shungite solution proved effective in managing conditions and reducing medication among 154 COPD patients. When asked if Shungite could help with respiratory problems Cassie referred to these findings and suggested inhaling Shungite steam by placing a bowl of boiling Shungite water under a towel. Within three days the first lady who tried this method no longer needed her inhaler and another acquaintance requested the instructions and found the same rapid relief.

The onset of a cold can be tough to handle when we are all busy people, but did you know that using Shungite steam inhalation can reduce the severity of cold and flu symptoms, which are also toxin detoxification symptoms. Additionally adding Shungite to a glass of tonic water can relieve headaches associated with colds within a couple of hours. Give these natural remedies a try and feel the difference in your body!

During a windy day Maggie was caught up in a whirlwind that swept her off her feet, causing her to fall to the ground. She sustained a severe injury to her forearm, and the area became swollen and purple and was likely to be broken. Due to a previous allergic reaction to plaster casts, she opted to stay at home and use a small piece of Elite Shungite stone instead. She was amazed to find that the swelling and purple bruising disappeared overnight. Within just ten days her arm had fully recovered.

Maggie also carried Shungite powder in her purse, she found that her bus pass was affected, and had to remove it from her purse to use it. Maggie shared with Oraphim that she engages nightly in interdimensional travel and found that the portals did require closing for her safe passage. She found Shungite was assisting this vital process because she required protection from being tracked. It is possible that the Shungite sensed her need for special protection as it seemed to help her avoid being tracked in all realms including the earthly realm of her waking day as her bus pass has an RFID tracking chip in it!

Amazing Balm Testimonial time from Tina!:

I have been "secretly " using your rescue balm on the fella. He has a various medical conditions, one being a Fibromyalgia sufferer. I've been rubbing onto areas that flare, he's mostly been asking for knees. He finally asked… what is that stuff it's bloody good! 😀

Now whilst I'm sorting his knees he says oh just do my feet and I just do my spine and oo just do my kidney area! He's blown away by the results and deffo had his interest pipped.

I finally shared with him about Shungite, what it does, and other stuff used for and why the pyramid and magnets and pendant etc are placed in certain areas and he was like well I like it, he's even said the house feels better and he's not having "those" nightmares!

As a light worker myself it has deffo kept the gremlins at bay and I cannot wait to give you more feedback once I get back out there busting gremlins and clearing etc.

Review From Stephen Koncar:

You was at Elsecar craft fair where I saw you and Richard and was very intrigued in the Shungite, that it was something new, I use healing crystals and charge them on my selenite and smudge them with sage but your healing items are much more beneficial to me as I put the easy earthers stickers in my trainers and I said that I had plantar fasciitis and since having these in they have worked wonders as I know have no pain, I have taken the toggles off the taps and put them around both mine and Tracey's water bottles, I have also used the balm on a scratch that I had on my hand and wow! The effects blew me away I will be hopefully ordering more toggles, EMF stickers, The balm and a shower head soon I'm just going to stick with drinking out of the drinks bottle with the toggle for now and every day like you said 100ml of the Shungite water that has the stone in.

Chris wrote:

"I feel it is more of letting you know about mine and my family's experience so far.

We bought it from you through your store after seeing your informative video at a Q&A you were doing at an expo type event I think? A little bit of previous research and a friend of mine has one of your stickers on the back of their phone had us pulling the trigger. A little bit like when you buy your first set of barefoot shoes you have to trust the manufacturer's information as it goes against what you previously knew about shoe purchasing, until you put them on. So I was slightly sceptical about what it might do for me even though

I know the Russians do not invest in just anything to the extent that you said in the video unless there is something to gain from it. I will jump to receiving and using the items. Myself and my other half noticed after about 20 mins to half an hour of wearing our triangle and tear-drop pendants respectively. We had an unexplained lack of tension in our bodies, like old Mr Soft from the mint advert but obviously not flopping all over the place. Our kind and quality of sleep since wearing them has been night and day better. Haven't been waking up with heavy eyelids and feeling half a step behind my body. We have felt a general level of peacefulness."

Chris continues: "I am titling this section Tinnitus because it has had quite a profound effect on the pair of us. I am a self-inflicted tinnitus owner; my other half had the more normal route a non-musician gets a ringing in their ears from. But here is where we had the real problem. The summer of 2022 we both started getting intermittent high pitch whining, like the 60 Hz cycle hum in our ears. Mine was having two pitches of tinnitus, two octaves above each other going off in my head. Each pitch had its distinctive areas of my ear where the pitches sat. Then New Year's Eve/New Year's Day 2022/23 it became permanent; two octaves ringing in my ears, that only abated when we went to bad or low mobile signal areas. When I noticed the effect of the necklace I thought I had gone deaf but it was actually part of my hearing not being pricked any-more. So my tinnitus hasn't gone and 60 Hz cycle hasn't either but the noise does just sit in one part of my ear and is a higher pitch than it used to be. When we could get our child to wear their necklace there was quite a dramatic change in their anxious behaviour, same thing when we could get them to wear the shoe laminated insole stickers. Living in a notoriously hard water area we have noticed how it has helped our water taste, dare I say soft. The stickers have also done what was said they would." Chris.

When it comes to reading scientific claims, it is often difficult to determine whether the results can be replicated at home. However, time and time again Shungite has proven to us that it can transform ourselves and our loved ones in very simple and effective ways. All we need to do is give Shungite the chance to demonstrate its capabilities, ask what it can do for you and allow the transformation to happen, *expect miracles.*

ACKNOWLEDGEMENTS

With very special thanks to Susie Ashworth,
Victoria Billingham and Rich Spray for
all their wonderful Shungite Partnerships.
Solly and Rich you are forever in my heart and
soul, you bring me the learning, development and
encouragement my spirit needs every day, thank you.

I am truly thankful for the contributions, insights and support
to bring this book to print from Nancy LHopkins, Veda Austin,
Kevin Doe, Chris Quartermaine, Jo Murphy, Roberta Beer, Andrea
Station, The Brews, David Rusby, Universal Kids, Ladan Ratcliffe,
Oliver Perceval, all the past, present and future Oraphim team
members, the team at Self Publishing.com and Susie Sykes.
And it is with great thanks to *you* for
wanting to know about Shungite.

AUTHOR BIO

Cassie's early career focused on grassroots creativity, community well-being and art education whilst also raising her son Solly, during her part time studies in Art and Design at Worthing College she was naturally drawn to researching the esoteric and obscure scientific aspects of metaphysical teachings mixed with spiritual insights from both the New Age 'hippy' culture and Christian perspectives resulting in a strong commitment to daily communing with her Creator. Her inventive and practical nature, combined with her passion for the creative arts and community teaching propelled her to spread joy among people of all ages and abilities.

Rich's awakening occurred whilst working in the obstetrics and gynaecological departments as an Operating Theatre Technician; during his 15 years in this role he had calmly and gently prepared patients for life saving operations in a highly stressful environment. He developed the skill of releasing fear and anxiety more rapidly than the anaesthetist could administer the appropriate calming drugs. His work also included the vital function of repairing electrical medical tools and preparing theatres with the appropriate equipment for operations. In his free time Rich created many proof-of-concept electrical devices that explored the movement of electrical energy, including tuning electricity into higher frequencies with Bedini circuits and Tesla coils.

Rich also played lead guitar in the rock band 'I Pariah' and combined his love for music with his passion for spiritual development and healing by developing music as a healing modality. He successfully removed 'voices' from mentally ill patients with his unique tunings and gentle guitar compositions. Rich created frequency healing meditations at events, which led to his feature on 'The Healing Sounds of Music' BBC Radio Sheffield. He sees a future role for himself in this area.

Both Cassie and Rich struggled with the academic side of school education due to dyslexia. As heart centred creative individuals, they both witnessed the limitations of mainstream options in the teaching and medical professions. They were becoming in resonance with each other's frequency with a matching up of desires, they both had a yearning to be of service and create solutions to address the challenges faced by so many, using their creative talents to the fullest extent.

Now their combined knowledge and creative skills produce powerful Shungite solutions for health and wellbeing that are also unique and beautiful - just like *YOU* their reader. In 2015 Cassie packed up her digital print and multimedia project studio, and together with Rich, they headed out of Sheffield, UK. Cassie had been a creative collaborator for over 20 years with many community projects, academics, doctors, and professors based at Sheffield University, but for now the void needed to be created for the prayer to be answered, and it did not take too long for the miracles to begin.

Cassie's latest book "SHUNGITE: Expect Miracles" is a must have for anyone on the spiritual path, anyone interested in quantum healing for themselves, their family and their friends. This magical mineraloid Shungite came from the Stars to help Humanity at this critical time as Cassie explains. This is The Bio Energetic Handbook for Surviving and Thriving in the 21st Century as we go through the Doorway of the Age of Aquarius and the limitless possibilities of The New Earth..3.2.2024

Roberta Beer

URGENT PLEA
Thank You for Reading My Book!

I really do appreciate your feedback and I love hearing what you have to say on your experiences with Shungite and also your journey through my book.

Please take two minutes now to leave a helpful review on Amazon letting me know what you thought of the book:

www.shungiteexpectmiracles.me

Thank You So Much

- Cassie

selfpublishing.com

Printed in Great Britain
by Amazon